SHARED GOVERNANCE, LAW, AND POLICY IN HIGHER EDUCATION

Publication Number 6

AMERICAN SERIES IN STUDENT AFFAIRS PRACTICE AND PROFESSIONAL IDENTITY

Edited by

NAIJIAN ZHANG, Ph.D.

West Chester University
Department of Counselor Education
West Chester, Pennsylvania

SHARED GOVERNANCE, LAW, AND POLICY IN HIGHER EDUCATION

A Guide for Student Affairs Practitioners

By

GEORGE S. MCCLELLAN

and

NEAL H. HUTCHENS

(With Contributions from Valeria Ross)

CHARLES C THOMAS • PUBLISHER, LTD.
Springfield • Illinois • U.S.A.

Published and Distributed Throughout the World by

CHARLES C THOMAS • PUBLISHER, LTD.
2600 South First Street
Springfield, Illinois 62704

ISBN 978-0-398-09352-5 (paper)
ISBN 978-0-398-09353-2 (ebook)

Library of Congress Catalog Card Number: 2020048111 (print)
2020048112 (ebook)

With THOMAS BOOKS *careful attention is given to all details of manufacturing and design. It is the Publisher's desire to present books that are satisfactory as to their physical qualities and artistic possibilities and appropriate for their particular use.* THOMAS BOOKS *will be true to those laws of quality that assure a good name and good will.*

Printed in the United States of America
MM-C-1

Library of Congress Cataloging-in-Publication Data

Names: McClellan, George S., author. | Hutchens, Neal H., author.
Title: Shared governance, law, and policy in higher education : a guide for student affairs practitioners / by George S. McClellan and Neal H. Hutchens.
Description: Springfield, Illinois : Charles C Thomas, Publisher, Ltd., 2021. | Series: American series in student affairs practice and professional identity ; publication number 6 | Includes bibliographical references and index.
Identifiers: LCCN 2020048111 (print) | LCCN 2020048112 (ebook) | ISBN 9780398093525 (paperback) | ISBN 9780398093532 (ebook)
Subjects: LCSH: Student affairs services–United States. | Student participation in administration–United States.
Classification: LCC LB2342.92 .M44 2021 (print) | LCC LB2342.92 (ebook) | DDC 371.4–dc23
LC record available at https://lccn.loc.gov/2020048111
LC ebook record available at https://lccn.loc.gov/2020048112

Dr. Margaret J. Barr (June 20, 1940 ~ June 7, 2018)

Dr. Margaret J. Barr, or Peggy as she was called by her many friends and colleagues, was a truly remarkable person. She was a woman executive officer at a major university at a time when that was rare. She held substantial leadership roles in both ACPA and NASPA. She was a scholar/practitioner well before the term came to common use. She was a mentor and role model to thousands of student affairs professionals, including some of the most influential people in our field. She made a positive difference in the lives of hundreds of thousands of college students through her service as a student affairs professional, her leadership in our professional associations, and her presentations and publications. People appropriately use words like icon and legend when describing her and the contributions she made to student affairs.

On a personal note, Peggy was a supervisor, mentor and role model, co-author and co-presenter, co-conspirator, consigliere, counselor, confidante, and friend to George. This book was to have been another of their shared projects. George and Peggy had some early discussions about how it might be helpful to student affairs professionals and what its contents might be, but Peggy's health issues took their toll before the two could fully develop the work together.

This book is dedicated to Peggy in appreciation for all that she shared with students, student affairs professionals, and the field of student affairs and with George's tremendous gratitude and love. The authors suspect she is already busily helping to organize the angels and supporting them in their holistic angelic development.

AUTHORS' NOTES

Believing for a number of years that many in higher education, including a number of colleagues in student affairs, do not have a full appreciation or understanding of shared governance and its value in American higher education, George invited Dr. John Levin, a colleague from his days at the University of Arizona, to author a chapter for the 3rd edition of the *Handbook of Student Affairs Administration* on the importance of shared governance to student affairs. Entitled "Institutional Governance and the Interests of Students." That chapter, which appeared in 2009, and an edited volume by Miller and Nadler (2006) stand nearly alone when it comes to professional literature focused specifically on the importance of shared governance to the work of those in student affairs.

This book seeks to fill this void. It provides information on the historical, philosophical, and legal foundations for shared governance, including both the more commonly understood albeit more narrowly focused construct of shared governance and the role of faculty and a more expansive understanding of shared governance to include boards of trustees/regents, various governance groups (students, staff, and faculty), alumni groups, community advisory boards, and others. It makes the link between fundamentals of law, policy, and shared governance as related to professional practice in student affairs. Finally, the book offers practical insights and suggestions for student affairs practitioners at all levels (entry-, mid-, and senior-) regarding how to work with shared governance groups and how to foster their success to help assure student and institutional success.

OVERVIEW

Chapter One offers definitions and common understandings of shared governance, its history in American higher education, and relevant theories and models. The chapter takes note of some contemporary developments and challenges related to shared governance and also briefly addresses some of the calls for revamping shared governance.

Chapter Two presents the common structures of shared governance from those with the broadest span of interest and authority to those with the narrowest. As each of the various structures is described and discussed, the stakeholders whose interests are represented by the structures are identified.

Chapter Three focuses on the ways in which we in higher education (and particularly in student affairs professional positions) can help foster and strengthen shared governance. It offers advice and suggestions for action in just that endeavor.

Chapter Four shares a brief history of student participation in shared governance as well as information on the degree to which students are (or are not) involved in shared governance in contemporary practice. Strategies are proffered for making the case for greater student involvement, and information is shared on the potential benefits to students from participating in shared governance. Additionally, strategies are identified for working directly with students to encourage and support them in taking part. The chapter concludes by presenting several important open questions about students and shared governance in American higher education.

Chapter Five explicates sources of law related to student affairs work. Rather than spending a great deal of time on case law, the chapter ties awareness of sources of the law, areas of law, and law-making processes to the conduct of shared governance.

Chapter Six discusses the individual role in shared governance. It specifically addresses the tension between the roles of institutional employee and private citizen.

Chapter Seven describes the policy arena and policy-making processes. Like Chapter Five, the focus here is centered on the ways in which the formation of policy and policy itself play out with regard to the intersection of student affairs and shared governance.

Chapter Eight draws together themes from throughout the preceding chapters. It also offers some closing thoughts on the importance of shared governance in American higher education and suggests a number of action items for student affairs professionals and others interested in strengthening governance at their institutions.

PURPOSE AND GOALS

Our goal in presenting this work is for readers to come away from the book with a better understanding of and appreciation for shared governance, law, and policy as well as an enhanced set of skills and strategies for engaging in shared governance as a matter of professional performance. Through fostering knowledge and abilities related to shared governance, the book assists readers in developing and forming their professional identity as well as in achieving learning outcomes aligned with specific professional practice standards in our field, including both the *CAS Professional Standards for Higher Education* (Council for the Advancement of Standards, 2015) and the ACPA/NASPA *Professional Competency Areas for Student Affairs Educators* (2015, available for review at https://www.naspa.org/images/uploads/main/ACPA_NASPA_Professional_Competency_Rubrics_Full.pdf).

Toward this end, case studies and reflective questions are featured throughout the book. An effort has been made to include examples from a variety of institutional settings in the discussion. However, the reader is encouraged to keep in mind the observation of Tip O'Neill, former Speaker of the United States House of Representatives, that all politics is local (O'Neill, 1995). The same is certainly true of shared governance.

INVITATION TO SHARE

Hopefully you will find this book informative and helpful as you work to support your students and your institution. Please feel free to share your experiences and feedback with us. Both are welcomed.

FOREWORD

Good governance is the art of putting wise thought into prudent action in a way that advances the well-being of those governed.
—Diane Kalen-Sukra

Finding the best authors for each volume of the *American Series in Student Affairs Practice and Professional Identity* has been a challenge. While collaborating with Dr. Mary F. Howard-Hamilton on a book project I mentioned the need to identify authors for the book on governance, law, and policy. Dr. Hamilton immediately recommended Dr. George McClellan would be a perfect fit to write this book. I was impressed by Dr. McClellan's background, his remarkable scholarship and rich experience in student affairs and higher education. I was hoping he would accept the invitation to write this book though he had his priorities and other commitments. I was excited when I heard he accepted my invitation and was willing to work on it. He further indicated that Dr. Margaret Barr would join him as the coauthor. I became more excited because I got to know Dr. Margaret Barr while I was a graduate student at Bowling Green State University during the early 1990s. However, unexpected news came that Dr. Barr became very ill and passed away in June 2018. I felt very sad that the profession of student affairs in higher education had a huge loss. Dr. Barr's sickness slowed the progress of this book, but I feel motivated to see the continuation of Dr. Barr's legacy with Dr. Neal Hutchens joining the project.

Dr. McClellan is a prominent scientist and practitioner who has published numerous books and articles and held vital administrative positions at both private and public institutions. His books, *Budgets and Financial Management in Higher Education* (2011 & 2018) with Margaret Barr, and *The Handbook for Student Affairs Administration* with J. Stringer (2009 & 2016), have been published in multiple editions, which reflect the popularity and value of these works. Besides publishing high quality articles and books, Dr. McClellan has served on the editorial board of the *Journal of College Student Development* and the *Journal of College and Character*. Moreover, Dr. McClellan has held high level administrative positions as vice chancellor for student affairs at Indiana University-Purdue University Fort Wayne and vice president for student development at Dickinson State University in Dickinson. He also held multiple leadership positions in the National Association of Student Personnel Administration (NASPA) and was recognized by the NASPA Foundation as a Pillar of the Profession in 2010 and in 2020 with the George D. Kuh Outstanding Contribution to Literature and Research Award. If we agree with Diane Kalen-Sukra that good governance is the art of putting wise thought into prudent action in a way that advances the well-being of those governed, Dr. McClellan is the artist who has created the art of good governance.

Dr. Neal Hutchens is a well-established scholar in law and policy of higher education. He has made significant contributions in law and shared governance to American higher education. He has published numerous research articles in professional journals and coauthored the sixth edition of *The Law of Higher Education and the Contested Campus: Aligning Professional Values, Social Justice, and Free Speech.* In addition, he has served on a significant number of editorial boards of professional journals in law and policy. All his knowledge and expertise in law and shared governance has greatly enhanced the value of *Shared Governance, Law, and Policy in Higher Education: A Guide for Student Affairs Practitioners.*

I appreciate both authors' knowledge, wisdom, and commitment to this book. Their footsteps in the field of higher education and student affairs have spoken well about them as true scientist-practitioners who have made significant contributions to the development of the American higher education and the American society in general. Therefore, I strongly recommend to you their book *Shared Governance, Law, And Policy in Higher Education: A Guide for Student Affairs Practitioners.*

Shared Governance, Law, and Policy in Higher Education: A Guide for Student Affairs Practitioners by Dr. George S. McClellan and Dr. Neal Hutchens is a book that will introduce you the key components of shared governance, law, and policy relevant to higher education and invite you to become a competent practitioner with a professional identity. A unique value of *Shared Governance, Law, and Policy in Higher Education: A Guide for Student Affairs Practitioners* is its unusual focus and integration. Its thematic and comprehensive chapters have presented not only a variety of important theories and models of shared governance but also action items such as advice, strategies, skills, and solutions on how to strengthen and create good governance at different institutions.

Throughout the entire book you will come to understand that shared governance, law, and policy are a fundamental part of student affairs practice in higher education and an ethical part of becoming competent student affairs educators. The worthy takeaways for readers include the history of shared governance in American higher education, the common structures of shared governance, relevant theories and models, history of student participation in shared governance, and strategies on how to encourage and support students for participation in shared governance in contemporary practice of student affairs in higher education. One essential aspect of the book is the advice and suggestions for readers' action in fostering and strengthening shared governance in their everyday practice as student affairs educators. Another unique aspect of the book is that it elucidates sources of law related to student affairs work and law-making processes to the conduct of shared governance. In addition, policy-making and policy implementations involving student affairs and shared governance are prescribed. Most importantly, the book ascribes what role you as a student affairs educator would play in shared governance.

Finally, *Shared Governance, Law, and Policy in Higher Education: A Guide for Student Affairs Practitioners* reveals the three common themes of the series with all other volumes in the *American Series in Student Affairs Practice and Professional Identity:* (1) integration of ACPA/NASPA Competency Areas for Student Affairs Educators; (2) development of professional identity; and (3) application of knowledge and theories to practice. Particularly, to reflect the theme of applying knowledge and theories to practice, this book has included numerous case studies and thought-provoking questions on governance, law, and policy to help student affairs educators to analyze complex governance issues that they may face in their daily practice. This book is a valuable tool which not only assists graduate students in student affairs preparation programs and new student affairs educators to expand their knowledge on governance issues in student affairs but also provides them with insights to develop their collaboration skills in working toward common ground – shared governance.

The *American Series in Student Affairs Practice and Professional Identity* is a unique book series that creates an integration of all ten professional competency areas for student affairs educators outlined by the College Student Educators International (ACPA) and the Student Affairs Administrators in Higher Education (NASPA) in 2015. The series reflects three major themes: professional competencies development, professional identity construction, and case illustrations for theory translation into practice. All volumes in the series are targeting graduate students in student affairs preparation programs and new student affairs educators. The series blends contemporary theories with current research and empirical support and uses case illustrations to facilitate the readers' ability to translate what they have learned into practice and decision making. Each volume focuses on one area of professional competency except the volume *College Students and Their Environments:*

Understanding the Role Student Affairs Educators Play in Shaping Campus Environments which addresses some major aspects of the Interaction of Competencies. As being said the series helps graduate students in student affairs preparation programs and new student affairs educators develop their professional competencies (ACPA/NASPA) by (1) constructing their personal and ethical foundations; (2) understanding the values, philosophy, and history of student affairs; (3) strengthening their ability in assessment, evaluation, and research; (4) gaining knowledge, skills, and dispositions relating to law, policy, and governance; (5) familiarizing with and learning how to effectively utilize organizational and human resources; (6) learning leadership knowledge and developing leadership skills; (7) understanding oppression, privilege, power, and then learning how to understand social justice and apply it in practice; (8) acquiring student development theories and learning how to use them to inform their practice; (9) familiarizing themselves with technologies and implementing digital means and resources into practice; and (10) gaining advising and supporting knowledge, skills and dispositions. As a result, the series helps graduate students in student affairs preparation programs and new student affairs educators foster their professional identity and ultimately achieve their goal of the whole-person education.

Naijian Zhang, Ph.D.
West Chester University of Pennsylvania

ACKNOWLEDGMENTS

George McClellan is appreciative to Dr. Naijian Zhang for the invitation to present this book for publication and for his patience and support throughout its development. Similarly, thanks are due to the team at Charles C Thomas, Publisher for bringing this book to its readers.

Tremendous thanks to Neal Hutchens for agreeing to join in this project. He has generously shared of his expertise in matters of law, policy, and shared governance to make this a better book. I am also grateful for his support as the chair of my department at the University of Mississippi and for his friendship.

I am also thankful to my colleagues in Higher Education and in the School of Education at the University of Mississippi. Their willingness to bring me into their number and their good cheer and strong support throughout the transition into full-time faculty life have been invaluable.

The students are always the best part of our work in higher education, and my experience is no exception to that rule. Thanks to all the students who have allowed me to be a part of their journey, either directly or indirectly, in higher education. I am particularly grateful to the Higher Education students at Ole Miss who challenge and inspire me with their commitment, compassion, and curiosity.

Early in the life of this project Peggy Barr and I agreed that we would invite a doctoral student from the University of Mississippi's Higher Education program to help us bring the manuscript forward. Peggy and I believed that our work would benefit from the inclusion of an emerging scholar practitioner and that the individual selected might benefit from the experience of helping bring a book to press. We were delighted when Valeria Ross expressed an interest in joining us. Unfortunately for both Peggy and Valeria, they never got the chance to work with one another. They both would have enjoyed sharing that very much. Valeria has provided tremendous assistance with this manuscript. She helped identify and review relevant literature, shared in conversations about various ideas included in the content, and provided useful feedback on early drafts of manuscript. I am grateful to her for the collegial assistance and support she has provided. I hope every faculty colleague is lucky enough to have students like Valeria in their programs.

Beyond the experience of writing this book, there are so many people who have helped me in innumerable ways throughout my lifetime. Among them, though certainly not all of them, are Yvonne Broske (my mother) and Howard McClellan (my father), Ken Christmon, Krissy Creager, Steve Grud, Jason Laker, Jeff Maher, Jason Meriwether, Jeff Sun, Joe Minonne, Chad Richmond, the Riffmaster and the Rockme Foundation nation, and Koko Taylor.

I also want to acknowledge the McIlhenny family for the gift of Tobasco sauce, the Brennan family in New Orleans for Commander's Palace, whoever is responsible for partnering grits with shrimp and with cheese for the joy of it all, and the folks at Walt's Chevron in Oxford for incredible plate lunches and pimento cheese sandwiches. Y'all make me smile.

Finally, thanks to all those who give of their time and talents to help make shared governance work on their campuses. Your efforts truly make a difference!

Neal Hutchens

I appreciate the generous offer from George McClellan to join him on this project. I also cannot say enough kind words about my other colleagues in the University of Mississippi Department of Higher Education and their friendship, support, and goodwill. Having the opportunity to work with them in launching the UM Department of Higher Education has proven a professionally fulfilling journey and provided the opportunity to reflect on fundamental aspects of higher education, including in the shared governance realm.

One of the most rewarding parts of my job is the privilege of working with outstanding students. Even when I am (often) disappointed by colleges and universities in failing to live up to their advertised institutional values and mission statements, including in matters of shared governance, I continually draw inspiration and hope from these talented and dedicated students.

I have been fortunate to have a number of gifted and supportive colleagues in my academic journey. I want to give a special acknowledgement to John Thelin of the University of Kentucky, a leading historian of higher education. During my career, John has been a constant source of support and encouragement. Thank you, John!

Finally, deep thanks are due to my partner in crime, Kelli Hutchens, for her support on this and many other projects. Clay and Elaina are our most important collaboration, and these two always keep me on my toes and remind me what is really special in life.

CONTENTS

ILLUSTRATIONS

SHARED GOVERNANCE, LAW, AND POLICY IN HIGHER EDUCATION

Chapter 1

OVERVIEW OF SHARED GOVERNANCE

The variety and complexity of the tasks performed by institutions of higher education produce an inescapable interdependence among governing board, administration, faculty, students, and others. The relationship calls for adequate communication among these components, and full opportunity for appropriate joint planning and effort.
American Association of University Professors (1967, ¶7)

Any conversation worth having about the strengths and challenges of American higher education will include discussion of one of its defining features–shared governance. However, as Levin (2009, p. 55) observes, "To state the governance of higher education institutions–either the understanding of the concept of governance or the practice of governing–is straightforward and without considerable complexity is to ignore the multiple strands of discourse and the experience of practitioners during the past several decades." Lizzio and Wilson (2009) add, "The ways in which institutions should be governed, and the roles of various parties in the process, are an enduring and often contested area of both practice and inquiry" (p. 69). Bahls (2014) succinctly stated, "Shared governance is one of the basic tenets of higher education, and yet there is considerable evidence that it is not generally understood by its primary participants–faculty members, presidents, and members of boards of trustees" (p. 1). The following case study illustrates the ways in which some of the complexities and challenges related to shared governance can play themselves out on a college campus.

Tough Times and Troubled Waters at Some State Regional University (SSR)

Some State Regional University (SSR), a public regional comprehensive institution in the Rust Belt, has enjoyed a number of years of enrollment growth, constructive relationships with the communities it serves, reasonable raises for employees, and generally positive campus morale and community regard. Much of this has come about during the service of a strong campus president who has been highly involved in almost every aspect of campus decision-making throughout her tenure until her retirement last year. Now, just as the new president is gaining her understanding of the SSR campus and community, a number of troubling circumstances are presenting themselves. Enrollments, which had stagnated toward the end of the previous president's service, have begun to shrink. This has put considerable pressure on the operating budget of the institution, and a hiring freeze and travel limitations have been instituted by the senior administrative leadership. No raises are going to be available for the coming year. Discussion of the enrollment challenges have also led to conversations with community leaders, including regional business people, indicating a dissatisfaction with the availability and quality of graduates from SSR as well as a lack of consultation regarding possible innovations in the curriculum to meet the emerging needs of the area's economy.

In response the budgetary challenges and the critique from the community, the new president establishes an ad hoc committee to develop a plan for revitalizing the curriculum of SSR with the goal of meeting regional needs, assuring institutional fiscal viability, and positioning the institution to fulfill the future needs of the community while raising its institutional profile and reputation. Given the focus on the future and on curricular realignment, the president wants to be sure to get new voices involved in this ad hoc group and so she solicits nominations from faculty and community groups for her consideration, a process which had been utilized on previous occasions by her predecessor when forming groups to consider issues or opportunities at SSR. Following review of the nominations by she and her cabinet, the president announces the new members of this blue ribbon ad hoc committee which will submit its report to the cabinet for review.

How do you think the president's plan will be received at SSR? What concerns regarding shared governance do you see being raised, if any, by the various stakeholders in this issue?

Likely the tenor and tone of the reactions at SSR would be shaped by the roles of those involved in the interaction and by their individual understanding of what exactly it is they have in mind when they speak about shared governance. So it is with this book, which I hope will unfold as a discussion amongst colleagues who care deeply about American higher education and in particular about student learning and student success in that context. Our conversation will draw on the literature of higher education and, where offered, our observations, opinions, and recommendations which are informed by our experiences as students, student leaders, student affairs professionals, institutional executive officer, and most recently as faculty members whose scholarship and teaching focuses on higher education, student affairs, and student learning and success. It is appropriate at this point to acknowledge our belief in the value of shared governance in American higher education, a belief which will become evident as we move forward through the chapters of this book if it has not already become apparent.

This chapter will address definitions and common understandings of shared governance, its history in American higher education, and relevant theories and models. The chapter will take note of some contemporary developments and challenges related to shared governance and also briefly address some of the calls for revamping shared governance.

WHAT IS SHARED GOVERNANCE?

According to Lechuga (2004), "Shared governance is a unique characteristic of the U.S. higher education system; it is often misunderstood and difficult to define" (p. 95). Olson (2009) similarly observes *shared governance* is a term that "is often invoked but much misunderstood by both faculty members and many administrators" (¶1). He goes on to say the phrase "is so hackneyed that it is becoming what some linguists call an "empty" or "floating" signifier, a term so devoid of meaning it takes on whatever significance a particular speaker gives it at the moment. Once a term arrives at this point, it is essentially useless" (¶5).

While in agreement with Olson with regard to how commonly misunderstood the term is, we are more sanguine with regard to our collective ability to restore vigor to both the term and the practice to which it refers. An important first step in a shared effort toward that end is to develop a definition of shared governance for the purposes of our work. Definitions of shared governance vary across the literature of higher education. The definitions proffered commonly refer to the structure (who is involved in the sharing and in what mechanisms), what is its purpose (what it is that is to be governed), the process through which it is to be pursued (how it will transpire), or some combination of the structure, purpose, and process of the thing. Each of these ways of defining shared governance will be addressed in this section of the chapter.

Structure

According to Cowley (1980) "The word *government* has evolved from the Latin verb *gubernare,* "to steer." It denotes any social structure possessing de jure or de facto power to steer or direct, that is, to control the actions of the individuals and groups within its province" (p. 4). *De jure* power derives from a legal right (De jure, n.d.); de facto power is the product of practice (De facto, n.d.). Chapter Two will present an extended conversation on the stakeholders in shared governance, but here it is important to point out that all de jure power of shared governance derives from powers vested in the board of trustees responsible for the legal entity represented in the university as authorized by the state legislature (in the case of a public university) or as provided for in the articles of incorporation (in the case of a private institution) and as construed or constrained by relevant administrative or judicial rulings (Kaplin & Lee, 2006; Olson, 2009). The board may in turn delegate some of those powers to various officers or entities, for example to the president of the university or to a governance group such as the faculty senate, as a matter of explicit policy or through its practices.

A common, and one might suggest classical, structural definition of shared governance is that that it primarily involves the board, the president, and the faculty (Bahls, 2014). Additional groups who might be included in a more expansive definition, a view which informs the discussion in Chapter Two, include students, staff, alumni groups, advisory boards, associations, and others.

Purpose

For what reason does higher education chose to engage all these participants in decision-making? It certainly is not for reasons of simplicity or expedience as neither is an espoused strength of shared governance. Simply put, one purpose is decision-making. Indeed, in what some argue is the origin of the term's application to American higher education, Corson (1960) used the term *governance* to discuss shared decision making between administration and faculty. One might be tempted to extend the purpose to better decision making, but that answer begs the question what understanding of *better* do we have in mind? Do we mean that it leads us to the right or best answer? Is such a thing even possible given the diversity of purposes for which we as a society pursue higher education (Labaree, 1997)?

An argument can be made that we in higher education believe shared governance leads to better decision making for two reasons: accessing expertise and engaging shareholders (Schotz, 2007). Consistent with values articulated in the AAUP *Statement on Governing Colleges and Universities* (AAUP, 1967; see Appendix) and reflecting several of the theories which inform it contemporary construction and practice, shared governance brings together administrators, faculty, and students to draw on their expertise relative to various aspects of university life and operations. The shareholder construct situates presidents and administration at the top of a hierarchy and the various stakeholders as constituents providing feedback and input (Schotz, 2007). However, as Fish (2007) points out, the challenge of identifying and including stakeholders in shared governance is problematic in a number of ways.

The understanding of what constitutes expertise and of who holds it can and does evolve over time as can the understanding of who the stakeholders are that ought to be involved in shared governance. Olson (2009) notes, "Shared governance has come to connote two complementary and sometimes overlapping concepts: giving various groups of people a share in decision-making processes, often through elected representation; and allowing certain groups to exercise primary responsibility for specific areas of decision-making" (¶10). The two notions of expertise and shareholder engagement are not always readily aligned in the practice of shared governance. Reed (2017) rightly observes, "Shared governance as an ideal attempts to split the difference between expertise and democracy" (p. 429). This is evidenced in the tendency for students, staff, and contingent and non-tenure track faculty to be marginalized in the structures and processes of shared governance on many campuses in some, if not many, conversations. Expertise, as it relates to faculty in higher education, has commonly been related to research rather than to teaching or knowledge of a disciplinary domain. This is the basis for the argument that has historically disenfranchised contingent and non-tenure track faculty.

Birnbaum identifies another tension between two interests as the purpose for which higher education engages in shared governance. He asserts, "Governance is the term we give to the structures and processes that academic institutions invent to achieve an effective balance between the claims of the two different, but equally valid, systems for organizational control and influence. One system, based on legal authority, is the basis for the role of trustees and administration; the other system, based on professional authority, justifies the role of the faculty" (2004, p. 5). Put another way, rather than a tension between stakeholder interest and expertise, Birnbaum addresses the tension between legal authority and expertise.

Higher education also engages in shared governance for reasons other than the pursuit of better decision-making. Just as budgets convey something about the values of an institution (Barr & McClellan, 2018), so does its practices related to shared governance. These practices both announce and affirm cultural dimensions of the campus community to current members, new members, and non-members alike. "Governance can reflect the patterned behaviors and cultural values found within higher education institutions" (Levin, 2009, p. 45). In contrast to hard governance (a term defined later in this chapter), the term soft governance has been applied to this purpose. *Soft governance* reflects "concepts of how organizational cultures are created over time through the interaction of people and the cognitive processes through which people come to share perceptions and "make sense" of what they are doing" (Birnbaum, 2004, p. 10). In this way, soft governance is retrospective (Birnbaum, 2004).

Brinbaum (1989) specifically notes the role of faculty senates as symbolic. Crellin (2010, p. 76), speaking more globally, opines, "Shared governance is integral to the culture of the academy. It is part tradition, part tactic, and largely symbolic."

Process

Chapter Two will feature the stakeholders and structures of common in American higher education shared governance. Here we will focus on its processes, which are yet another way we can understand it. Birnbaum (2004, p. 10) describes this as *hard governance.* ""Hard" (or rational) governance refers to the structures, regulations and systems of sanctions in an organization that define authority relationships, prescribe certain organizational processes and encourage compliance with enacted policies and procedures" (Birnbaum, 2004, p. 10). He identifies rational choice, in which rational actors, weighing costs and benefits, arrive at decisions based on self-interest looking forward, as the philosophical underpinning of hard governance.

Kaplin (2004) argues, "Governance refers to the means and actions by which a collective entity decides matters of policy and strategy. . . . In general, the governance system is understood to consist of the explicit and implicit procedures that allocate to various participants the authority and responsibility for making institutional decisions" (p. 23).

Explicit procedures are those processes defined and described in governing documents of the institution and of its governance groups. Examples include articles of incorporation for the institution or its chartering document; institutional policy and procedure manuals; academic department procedures; and student, staff, and faculty senate constitutions and their bylaws.

Implicit procedures are those which are not expressly defined but which are inferred through interpretation or application of explicit procedures or which may be commonly understood as a function of custom or prior practice. Institutional documents may explicitly reference a commitment to shared governance, but they may be silent with regard to precisely how that consultation should be played out in some instances. For example, there may be a general statement about the importance of shared governance in an institutional charter. There may even be a general statement in institutional policy regarding the importance of appropriate consultation with stakeholders with regard to hiring senior academic or administrative personnel. However, it has been our experience that the exact nature of that consultation is more often premised on prior practice rather than a detailed policy or practice statement.

Regardless of whether explicit or implicit and hard or soft, shared governance may also be understood through an exploration of how it is that people conduct themselves in the course of engaging in it. In speaking about how shared governance is carried out, Levin comments,

> Scholars of governance in higher education usually offer one of two judgements on the behaviors of those involved in the process. One reflects a rather rational, well-ordered system in which there are rules, guidelines, and behavioral precedents established so that civilized exchanges occur between equals (Baldridge, Curtis, Ecker, and Riley, 1977: Hines, 2000). The other reflects a political process where power and contest are normal behaviors (Pusser, 2003). From this later perspective, concepts of governance are aligned with power, what Mintzberg (1983) and others refer to as the ability to realize intentions by influencing or convincing others to act. In organizations, various players form alliance in order to obtain desired results. (2009, p. 51)

According to Bejou and Bejou (2016, p. 56), "Shared governance is an integrate model of governance in which the administration, academic units, and representative governing bodies (administrators, faculty, staff, and students) exist side by side in a mutually enhanced relationship of open communication, transparency, and true collaboration." This stands in stark contrast to Lachs' (2011) view that faculty are mostly driven by a narrow set of self-interests.

Combination

Of course, the divide between structure, purpose, and process is an artificial one used here for the purposes of bringing information forward. It is more often the case in actual practice that these aspects of understanding governance are interconnected and intertwined. Crellin (2010) offers, "Shared governance is both a means to an end and an end to be maintained and valued; it is a collaborative process while also an outcome of collegiality; it is steeped in tradition yet concerns itself with change and innovation in the academy; and most of all, it seeks to bridge difference and yet curiously exacerbates it" (p. 80). We find that Levin's nuanced description of shared governance resonates with our experiences in higher education.

> Institutional governance is on the one hand what shapes institutional behaviors and on the other hand what defines the character of the institution. Governance of higher education institutions both structures the actions of the institution and its members and give meaning to organizational action. That is, governance is both a verbal construct and a noun; it connotes action as well as condition. . . . Governance includes both how institutional behaviors and actions are carried out—the methods—and what actions are taken—the goals realized. (Levin, 2009, pp. 51–52)

HISTORY OF SHARED GOVERNANCE

Having explored what we mean when we speak of shared governance, attention now turns to how it is that we came to this place in time. This section will offer a brief history of shared governance in American higher education, noting key moments or turning points in the evolution of the construct in American higher education. Readers interested in a more detailed and robust recounting are encouraged to visit the sections on this history of shared governance in either Cowley's (1980) *Presidents, Professors, and Trustees or Gerber's (2014) The Rise and Decline of Faculty Governance: Professionalization and the Modern American University.*

Early Governance

The first principles of what has come to be known as shared governance were brought to the Colonies by early settlers and were premised on ideas at play in European tertiary education (Taylor & De Lourdes Machado, 2008). "The model of university governance that emerged within the United States was influenced in part by the Swiss Calvinist structure in the General Academy, and in part by the Scottish university approach to governing financial matters" (Austin &

Jones, 2016, p. 11). The key elements imported were the authority of a lay board of trustees, the position of a president, and the role of faculty in university life. Harvard College, what we now know as Harvard University, is the oldest college in the United States, and the model of having boards of lay members providing oversight for a president charged with responsibility for the institution can be traced back to its founding (Pusser & Loss, 2018). American colleges were relatively small with narrowly defined missions up to the later nineteenth century and the emergence of the modern university, and their governance featured strong presidents overseen by external boards (Gerber, 2014). Later, concurrent with the emergence of the participation of faculty in governance, was the development of system or statewide boards for public higher education. The first statewide board for four-year institutions was created in 1905 in Florida (Austin & Jones, 2016).

Emerging Role of the Faculty

Discussion of a faculty role in governance began in the mid-nineteenth century, and the practice slowly took root in the late nineteenth and early twentieth century. As institutions grew in their size and complexity and as the professoriate became more professionalized (Gerber, 2014), there began to be a call for a role for faculty in the governance of colleges. Birnbaum (2004) notes that the president of the University of Michigan was making the argument in 1858 that faculty should have authority over curricular matters and teaching methods given their unique expertise. "This principle, while broadly recognized, was honored more in the breach than in the observance by many institutions for the next fifty years. But the increasing professionalism of the faculty during the early decades of the twentieth century, accelerated by the academic revolution following World War II, led many institutions to accept not only faculty control over the curriculum but also a strong faculty voice in other education-related matters" (Birnbaum, 2004, p. 5).

Shared Governance and The AAUP Statement

The rapid expansion of American higher education after World War II, the continued growth in complexity of both individual institutions and in systems of higher education, shifts in societal expectations and understandings with regard to the role of higher education and the rights and responsibilities of various stakeholders in it, the earliest vestiges of what has come to be known as neoliberalism and the attendant external pressures on higher education, and the social change voiced in civil rights and anti-war movements of the 1960s all can be understood as having played an important contextual role in a watershed moment in the history of shared governance in American higher education–the adoption of the American Association of University Professors' (AAUP) *Statement on Government of Colleges and Universities* (AAUP, 1967). Jointly developed by the AAUP, American Council on Education (ACE), and the Association of Governing Boards of Universities and Colleges (AGB), the full text of the statement appears in the Appendix.

As noted in the document, "The statement is intended to foster constructive joint thought and action, both within the institutional structure and in protection of its integrity against improper intrusions" (AAUP, 1967, ¶1). The *Statement on Government of Colleges and Universities* (AAUP, 1967) articulates the purposes of shared governance, the participants in it, and the roles of those participants relative to governance. Chapter Two will focus on the latter two points so we will focus here on the former which is expressed in the document as advancing joint effort. This concept is described in the statement as follows:

> The general educational policy, i.e., the objectives of an institution and the nature, range, and pace of its efforts, is shaped by the institutional charter or by law, by tradition and historical development, by the present needs of the community of the institution, and by the professional aspirations and standards of those directly involved in its work. . . . The interests of all are coordinate and related, and unilateral effort can lead to confusion or conflict. (AAUP, 1967, ¶7)

The statement goes on to further operationalize the term by asserting, "Such matters as major changes in the size or composition of the student body and the relative emphasis to be given to the various elements of the educational and research program should involve participation of governing board, administration, and faculty prior to final decision" (AAUP, 1967, ¶12). Other internal operations of higher education institutions are also identified and addressed as part of joint effort and, hence, appropriately subject to shared governance. Among these other operations are: long-range planning, physical resources, budget, selection of the president and senior academic administrative leadership. It is interesting to note that no reference is made to senior administrative leaders such as chief financial officers, chief student affairs officers, or chief development officers. One could hypothesize that these roles were not then viewed by faculty and others as being essential or important ones in the life of the institution, but it is difficult to imagine in contemporary practice that an institution would seek to bring new people into these roles without campus consultation consistent with the practices of shared governance as described and exercised on that campus.

The *Statement on Government of Colleges and Universities* (AAUP, 1967) also identifies a right of a member of identified shared governance groups (limited though they may be in the statement) to address issues of concern relative to campus. Specifically, it states, "The right of a board member, an administrative officer, a faculty member, or a student to speak on general educational questions or about the administration and operations of the individual's own institution is a part of that person's right as a citizen and should not be abridged by the institution. There exist, of course, legal bounds relating to defamation of character, and there are questions of propriety" (AAUP, 1967, ¶20).

Recent Developments

The construct of shared governance as we know it today took rapid root following the adoption of the *Statement on Government of Colleges and Universities* (AAUP, 1967) and throughout the 1970s. The increasing complexity of rapidly expanding institutions and systems of higher education, rise of managerialism and neoliberalism, calls for accountability and increasing externalization of control, and deprofessionalization of the professoriate (all discussed in subsequent sections of this chapter) which can be traced to the late 1970s and continuing to current time have contributed to strains on the understanding and practice of shared governance. Most recently, the Association of Governing Boards has issued a series of reports on shared governance (2016, 2017) in which it addresses concerns regarding the functionality of shared governance structures and processes. While those reports have reaffirmed the *Statement on Government of Colleges and Universities* (AAUP, 1967) as a guiding document and shared governance as a foundational principle, they have opened the door to discussion of changes which some see as an enhancement and others as an assault.

Theories and Models

The AAUP *Statement on Government of Colleges and Universities* (AAUP, 1967) is a foundational document in understanding shared governance as practiced in American higher education, but that practice flows from and reflects a number of theories and models. Ausin and Jones argue, "An analysis of higher education governance in the USA must be grounded in conceptualizations that draw on formative cultural, political, socioeconomic, and historical underpinnings of the country. It is a country that is characterized by antistatism, individualism, populism, and egalitarianism" (2016, pp. 106–107). Austin and Jones (2016) go on to identify a number of theories which can be helpful in reflecting on shared governance, and their work informs much of the early portion of this section of the chapter.

Theories of Organizational Behavior

Theories of organizational behavior can be helpful in understanding governance issues related to state control, association or professional influence, and interactions with key stakeholders such as governmental agencies, private sector entities, or grant providers. Institutional theory and resource dependence theories are examples of two such theories of organizational behavior which reflect the prime motivation of all organizations, like all living organisms, to survive and thrive.

Institutional theory. Institutional theory can help "explain some of the governance structures and practices observed in universities-the coming together of isomorphism, legitimacy, and universities' environments" (Austin & Jones, 2016, p. 29). Isomorphism is the similarity of functions between like organisms or organizations. This similarity comes about as a result of the entities facing similar constraints, or it may be the result of purposeful copying. Dimaggio and Powell (1983) offer a classic discussion of isomorphic behavior in higher education institutions, noting that fields where definitions of quality and outcomes are vague are particularly prone to mimetic isomorphism. The same vagueness drives the question for legitimacy which consumes so much time and attention in higher education. Compounding the lack of clear, shared, and measurable notions of quality and outcomes is the openness of the higher education system. By openness, we mean that the boundary between the institutions and their environment are not closed (Bess & Dee, 2008); constituents and shareholders of various stripes seek to engage with and influence universities in many ways. "This has resulted in challenges to existing forms of governance and major shifts in how institutions are governed" as "universities seek to preserve or enhance their legitimacy by conforming to environmental pressures and are driven to adopt governance structures that fit with societal demands and expectations" (Austin & Jones, 2016, p. 29).

Resource dependence theory. Like institutional theory, resource dependence theory addresses the interaction between an organization and its environment. Specifically, resource dependence theory recognizes that the environment can shape organizational behavior "based on the assumption that organizations are dependent on their environment for critical resources and, as a result, organizations are controlled by and vulnerable to their environments" (Austin & Jones, 2016, p. 30). It is not simply the case, however, that the organization must accept the environment as is. There may be instances in which the organization seeks to bring about changes in the environment or to reshape its boundaries in ways that open up new lines for resources (Bess & Dee, 2008).

Theories of Transactional Behavior

Another group of theories can be helpful in understanding governance from the perspective of the transactional nature of the enterprise. How do the players involved in governance view themselves and others in the course of conducting business. Agency theory, stewardship theory, and stakeholder theory can offer insights in this regard.

Agency theory. There are two primary groups of constituents considered in agency theory–principals and agents. "The principals are the owners (shareholders in the case of a public corporation) and the agents are the managers/executives hired by the principals" (Austin & Jones, 2016, p. 34). Principals hire agents to run things in the best interest of the owners, but there may be times when the interests of the principals and the interests of the agents diverge. This misalignment of interests is referred to as the *agency problem* (Austin & Jones, 2016). Governance processes are established as a means to help monitor and control the agents at just such moments in time. While agency theory has seen relatively limited application in higher education, it may well be the case that it comes into wider favor as the organizational and governance structures in higher education become increasingly complex (more on that in the later section on contemporary developments).

Stewardship theory. Whereas agency theory is born of economics and assumes rational self-interest, stewardship theory is drawn from psychology and sociology and assumes that agents want to do well for the interests of the organization. They see themselves as stewards. "This does not mean that the interests of agents and principals will always be aligned, but simply that agents derive greater utility from cooperative behaviors and act in ways that promote cooperative interests at the expense of their self-interest" (Austin & Jones, 2016, p. 38). Stewardship theory reflects a collectivist notion (as opposed to the individualistic view of agency theory), and an agent facing conflicting interests from stakeholders will seek to satisfy competing claims (Austin & Jones, 2016). One reason that stewardship theory may be more commonly used to understand higher education behavior is *identification.* People drawn to serve in higher education are folks who believe there is merit in education broadly or in their specific discipline. "When stewards identify with the organization, they take on a membership relationship with the organization that enhances their willingness to pursue its mission, vision, and objectives" (Austin & Jones, 2016, p. 40).

Stakeholder theory. Stakeholder theory can be thought of as a bridge between institutional theory and agency theory in that it addresses those in the environment with interests and the ways in which they may engage in governance. As Austin and Jones (2016, pp. 42–43) explain, "external stakeholders are more than just governments that fund public universities. They include individuals from civil society and private organizations. . . . Stakeholder involvement in university governance is more related to responsiveness to society and the legitimacy of an institution in the eyes of the wider society represented by these multiple stakeholder groups."

Social exchange and justice theories. According to Birnbaum, "All governance institutions must deal with two issues: making good decisions and getting those subject to such systems to accept the decisions as legitimate" (2004, p 12). He goes on to explain,

> Social exchange theories assume that people will accept decisions in a calculative way in order to maximize their outcomes. Distributive

> justice theories also emphasize outcomes, but focus on the fairness with which resources are distributed and the degree to which personal benefits are appropriate. Procedural justice theories also emphasize fairness, but instead of looking at outcomes, the judgement is made based on the degree to which the procedures used to reach the directives are consistent with the values of the group. (Birnbaum, 2004, p. 13)

Models for Understanding Governance

In addition to the various theories already discussed, there are a number of models which may be helpful in understanding the practice of shared governance in American higher education. Austin and Jones (2016) identify six models, noting the primary characteristics of each. The six models are:

- Hierarchy–vertical relationship, coordination and control, managerial
- Bureaucracy–rationality, chains of command
- Organized anarchy–vague goals and technology
- Garbage can model–fluid participation, solutions looking for problems
- Politics/power–conflict, negotiation, cooperation based on self-interests, rewards; coercion
- Organization–environment relations; power uncertainty; strategic contingencies theory and resource-dependence theory

Contemporary Developments and Challenges

These theories and models which can inform our understanding and practice of shared governance have remained relatively unchanged since their articulation in the literature, but the circumstances under which those theories and models are applied and tested have changed greatly. Among the changes which have had the greatest implications for shared governance are shifts in student enrollment and student expectations; growth of the community college sector; increasing role of non-tenure track faculty; unionization (particularly of graduate students and faculty); emergence of private, for-profit institutions as a significant segment of higher education; increasing complexity of higher education organizational structures including expansion of systems of higher education, multiversities, globalization and mega-universities, and proliferation of state boards; and the increasing prevalence of neoliberalism and managerialism as driving forces in higher education policy at both the state and national level.

Student enrollment and expectations. It is not only changes in higher education institutions and structures which present challenges for traditional notions of shared governance. Changes in the students who are taking part in higher education and the ways in which they are taking part are also important to consider. Students are increasingly part-time, older, working in addition to taking classes, women, and members of minoritized populations. With regard to shared governance, these students bring with them varying expectations as well as interest in and availability to participate. All of this at a time when students overall are increasingly inclined to look to computer-mediated communication for opportunities to engage.

Community college sector. Joliet Junior College, established in 1901, was the first community college in the United States (Reed, 2017). According to the National Center for Educational Statistics (NCES) (2001) there were 752 2-year institutions of higher education in the United States in the year that the *Statement on Government of Colleges and Universities* (AAUP, 1967) was adopted. Four decades later there were 1,732 such institutions, an increase of 130 percent. The number of 4-year institutions during that same time grew from 1,577 to 2450, a substantial but more modest 55 percent (NCES, 2001).

The governance structures for community colleges vary from state to state (Reed, 2017) in much the same way that governance structures for public 4-year institutions vary. Given their historic reliance on contingent and non-tenure track faculty as well as their proximity to the marketplace and alignment with more managerial models of administration, shared governance has not been as central to institutional decision-making at community colleges as it has been at 4-year institutions. This is changing. As Reed (2017) observes, "Shared governance is a hotly contested topic throughout higher education in the United States, but the tensions surrounding it are in particularly stark relief in the community college sector" (p. 428). The increasing professionalization of the faculty in community colleges and greater managerial pressures (see the later discussion of neoliberalism in this section) has led to greater expectations on the part of community college faculty for more meaningful participation (Lucey, 2002).

Non-tenure track faculty. Another important change in American higher education has been the rapid expansion in the proportion of non-tenure track faculty (NTTF) members. Tenured and tenure track positions constituted 75% of faculty opportunities in the late 1970s; nearly two-thirds of those positions were held by non-tenure track faculty by the turn of the century "While NTTF, especially part-time NTTF, are largely concentrated in community colleges, growth trends can be seen across other higher education sectors as well" (Jones, Hutchnes, Hulbert, Lewis, & Brown, 2017, p. 507).

As noted in the earlier discussion regarding expertise, non-tenure track faculty have historically been marginalized with regard to participation in shared governance. One of the ways through which this marginalization has been enacted has been the ineligibility of non-tenure track faculty to serve as voting members of faculty senates. It has been argued that NTTF may be less inclined or able to speak freely in opposition to administrative policy or practices given the absence of job protections afforded to tenured faculty (Jones, Hutchnes, Hulbert, Lewis, & Brown, 2017).

With the rapid growth in representation of NTTF in faculty positions, there has been a substantial shift in their eligibility to participate in shared governance. Several studies in the early 2000s indicated less than 50 percent of higher education institutions permitted full-time NTTF to serve in their faculty senates; a similar study by Jones, Hutchnes, Hulbert, Lewis, and Brown about 15 years later showed that figure had risen to 85 percent of institutions (Jones, Hutchens, Hulbert, Lewis, & Brown, 2017).

Unionization. Unionization of faculty can be understood as a consequence of changes in the hiring, promotion, and management practices of higher education which have been increasingly driven by a managerial perspective. "This trend toward faculty unionization began in the late 1960s as a movement representing faculty issues and concerns such as salary increases. . . . In the United States 27 percent of all faculty . . . are represented by collective bargaining agreements" (Austin & Jones, 2016, p. 140).

Nicholas Burbules (2013) argues that faculty unionization hurts shared governance as it shifts the discourse from a constitutional framework, based on foundational documents and principles, to a contractual framework based on a negotiated contract. Rhoads (2011) counters that, given the increasing managerialism in higher education, the shift to a contractual perspective may be most beneficial to faculty in helping assure their rights in the university. Porter (2013) found that unionization had a positive relationship with faculty influence in some matters of shared governance, and Kater and Levin (2004) report unionized faculty in community colleges participate in shared governance in a number of meaningful ways.

Graduate student unionization, though to a lesser extent than for faculty, is also a concern related to matters of shared governance. According to Wickens (2008, p. 545),

> The most controversial group of academic union organizers consists of graduate students serving as research and teaching assistants. The movement to form graduate student unions has accelerated rapidly in the past 15 years. In 1990, there were five American graduate student unions. By the fall of 2000, graduate employees in 23 universities had voted to unionize, and in at least 19 other universities, graduate employees were in the process of organizing (Rhoades & Rhoads, 2002). Throughout the 1990s, membership in graduate student unions tripled to include almost 40,000 teaching and research assistants (DeCew, 2003). By 2006, there were more than 40 universities with recognized graduate student unions. (Singh et al., 2006)

Austin and Jones (2016) later noted fully 20 percent of graduate students employees are unionized.

Private, for-profit institutions. Though not as pronounced as the trends in the growth of the community college sector, proportion of faculty who are non-tenure track, or unionization in the academic work force, the changes in the number and structure of private, for-profit institutions do have implications for shared governance in American higher education. A common criticism of traditional shared governance is that it is time consuming and therefore hampers the ability of college and universities to respond quickly to emerging challenges or opportunities. A response to this perceived shortcoming that is becoming more common is for both public and private not-for-profit institutions to develop alternative for-profit arrangements which, while subject to accreditation and the attendant relatively modest requirements relative to shared governance (Barrett & Quarless, 2017), allow for the creation of processes which are seen as being less cumbersome. Examples of institutions engaging in such practices include Purdue, Cornell, University of Maryland Baltimore County, and Chapman (Ho, 2017).

Increasing complexity of organizational structures. In addition to the emergence of for-profit institutions, the growing complexity of organizational structures in higher education presents challenges to traditional forms of shared governance. The rapid expansion of enrollments following World War II led to growth in the number of higher education institutions, rise of the community college, and the emergence of multi-campus systems (Thelin, Edwards, & Moyen, 2018). A concomitant response on the part of states was to look to state boards to provide some form of control or oversight to what must have seemed to legislators at the time as a rapidly sprawling investment in infrastructure.

Not only were the systems of higher education becoming more complex, so too were individual institutions. Noted educator Clark Kerr coined the term *multiversity,* as opposed to university, to describe the emergence of higher education institutions with (Wagner, 2007), a broad set of functions, schools or colleges, and departments. These changes present challenges with regard to assuring the opportunity to participate to all stakeholders and in building consensus around goals and pathways to goals given the variety of disciplinary and bureaucratic perspectives at play.

The increase in complexity is not merely within state or even national borders. Higher education is increasingly globalized (Marginson, 2004) and corporatized (Burgan, 2004). Both have implications for shared governance in American higher education. With globalization has come the rise of *mega-universities.* Sir John Daniel coined the term mega-universities in the mid-1990s (Daniel, Kanwar, & Uvalic-Trumbic, 2005) in discussing the ways in which some number of institutions are now operating in significant ways across national boundaries in competing for resources and prestige. While not clearly or commonly defined (Blumenstyk, 2018), the term may be applied to institutions more aligned more with traditional business practices and principles than with those typically associated with higher education. These institutions emphasize the importance of being facile and innovative and commonly see the need to move beyond typical governance structures which are seen as cumbersome and slow. Southern New Hampshire University is an example of one such institution.

Most colleges claim academic considerations, not administrative culture or consumer-driven technology, as their raison d'être. At Southern New Hampshire, the instructional program gets its fair share of attention. But it's not the selling point. "We want an academic program that's like a Honda Accord," LeBlanc is fond of saying, nodding to the car's reputation for solid engineering and good value. "But we want to be the Nordstrom of student service and success" (Blumenstyk, 2018, ¶34–35).

With regard to corporatization, it is worth noting that the private sector also engages in governance. There are corporate boards, labor unions, and employee councils for many companies. The challenge, however, is that these corporate models of governance are not readily translated to a higher education setting. Collis (2004) describes five key differences in the two settings which make this so. They are:

1. Participants in higher education institutions are simultaneously pursuing multiple goals.
2. The outputs of higher education are difficult to evaluate.
3. Higher education governing bodies includes multiple conflicting constituencies.
4. Some constituents in higher education have veto power in some situations.
5. The absence of a strong hierarchy and weak incentives for faculty result in administrators having few tools with which to handle those not cooperating.

Neoliberalism and managerialism. Similar in some ways to corporatization, neoliberalism is "constructed around a market-driven rationality with an emphasis on individualism and ruthless completion and with a subtext that promotes a logic of privatization, efficiency, flexibility, the accumulation of capital, and the minimization of state action" (Austin & Jones, 2016, p. 166). Nef and Robles (as cited in Austin & Jones, 2016) list the following as tenets of neoliberalism:

- Re-establishing the rule of the market
- Reducing taxes
- Deregulating the private sector
- Reducing public expenditures
- Privatization of the public sector
- Elimination of the collectivist concept of "the public good"

Managerialism goes hand-in-hand with neoliberalism. "Managing" and "management" are core theses of managerialism, in which managing is a set of sociotechnical practice for rationality coordinating and controlling collective action, while management is the collective agents and institutions for responsible for enacting these practices" (Austin & Jones, 2016, p. 169). New public management (NPM) is a line of argument within managerialism which "holds sound or good governance is vital to economic development and societal advancement, and that the public sector should function on the basis of good governance" (Austin & Jones, 2016, p. 170). Austin and Jones (2016) observe, "The practices associated with NPM include performance measurement, customer and bottom-line orientation, the revising of incentive schemes, deregulation, outsourcing, and privatization" (p. 171). The tensions between the values of neoliberalist NPM and those associated with traditional notions of shared governance in higher education are stark and profound, and much of the frustrations regarding higher education expressed by state legislators, conservative education policy analysts, business interests, and other stakeholders reflect NPM ideology.

Calls for Change in Shared Governance

The developments and challenges just described, along with others which have taken place in the 50 years since the adoption of the AAUP *Statement on Government of Colleges and Universities* (AAUP, 1967), have occasioned criticism of shared governance in American higher education and corresponding calls for various changes in it. Schuster, Smith, Korak, and Yamada (1994) call for linking strategic planning and regular governance procedures, specifically proposeing strategic planning councils.

Lachs (2011), a former leader of a faculty senate, notes the degree of administrative influence (including academic administrators) on committees which, in the end, only offer recommendations. Birnbaum, drawing on the work of Gumport, describes a perceived fundamental tension related to shared governance between an academic-oriented higher education institution and a market-oriented one. "It was suggested earlier that shared governance may be important to the proper performance of an academic institution, but may be counterproductive in a market one. . . . If institutions become less academic, governance is less likely to be shared, and as governance is less shared, institutions are likely to become less academic" (2004, p 11).

Kaufman-Oborn (2016) notes the concerns raised about external forces intruding into higher education for various purposes and the attacks on tenure and shared governance said to be associated with those perceived intrusions. However, he also points to neoliberalism and careerism in the faculty (and the subsequent withdrawal from robust participation in shared governance) as a less-spoken about explanation for the diminishment of shared governance. Bejou and Bejou (2016), argue that changing roles and players is leading to "governance gridlock" (p. 54) and suggest, "given these external pressures, the traditional shared governance model is no longer a viable forum by which to make sound decisions in higher education. It is not designed to deal with multiple, demanding pressures in a timely fashion" (p. 55).

The recommendations to recast shared governance are as ubiquitous as the critiques. Kaufman-Osborn (2016) observes about the discussion regarding shared governance, "While all parties to this debate agree that higher education in the United States is now undergoing a profound transformation, opinions diverge on what this signifies for shared governance. The American Association of University Professors, for example, contends that a robust reaffirmation of the faculty's role is in order, while the Association of Governing Boards of Universities and Colleges, known as AGB, insists that meeting the imperatives of a new era requires acknowledgment and support of that role, but also considerable amplification of executive authority as well as enhanced trustee oversight" (¶2).

Birnbaum (2004) says many of the proposals to revamp shared governance focus on hard governance and that there is not much evidence that these efforts historically have had much of an impact. "While hard governance can channel and to some extent harness the power of soft governance, so that the two are mutually reinforcing, in and of itself it appears to have little influence" (p. 10). He goes on to observe, "Hard governance makes little difference because most of the important decisions made in the university occur outside the formal system. . . . Hard governance proposals almost always sound reasonable and self-evident. But when they conflict with soft governance, they inevitably fail. Soft governance rules!" (p. 11).

REFLECTION QUESTIONS

1. Using a 4-point scale where 4 is fully informed and 1 is fully uninformed, how would you assess your knowledge about shared governance prior to beginning to read this book? Where does your knowledge of shared governance come from (e.g., graduate program, experience as a student, or experience as a higher education faculty member or administrative staff member)?
2. What is your working definition of shared governance as it pertains to American higher education?
3. What do you see as the strengths and challenges associated with shared governance in higher education?
4. On the whole, do you see shared governance as helpful or harmful in American higher education?
5. What new information or insights about shared governance, if any, did you gain from reading this chapter, and how will you use the newfound information and insights moving forward to enhance your professional performance and development?

Chapter 2

SHARED GOVERNANCE SHAREHOLDERS AND STRUCTURES

Joint effort in an academic institution will take a variety of forms appropriate to the kinds of situations encountered. In some instances, an initial exploration or recommendation will be made by the president with consideration by the faculty at a later stage; in other instances, a first and essentially definitive recommendation will be made by the faculty, subject to the endorsement of the president and the governing board. In still others, a substantive contribution can be made when student leaders are responsibly involved in the process. Although the variety of such approaches may be wide, at least two general conclusions regarding joint effort seem clearly warranted: (1) important areas of action involve at one time or another the initiating capacity and decision-making participation of all the institutional components, and (2) differences in the weight of each voice, from one point to the next, should be determined by reference to the responsibility of each component for the particular matter at hand, as developed hereinafter.

American Association of University Professors (1967, ¶8)

Chapter 1 offered an overview of shared governance in U.S. higher education including various definitions, its history, underlying theories and models, contemporary challenges, and critiques. This chapter will offer a discussion of the structures which comprise shared governance and shareholders represented in these structures. The focus throughout will be on the structures and shareholders that student affairs practitioners might interact with at various points in their careers. Specifically, the discussion will include: governing boards;

boards of trustees; administration; senates (student, faculty, staff, and blended); unions; other student governance groups (for example, residence halls councils); advisory councils; alumni groups; and other groups.

Kaplin (2004) observes, "In higher education the powers allocated to faculty, to the public's representatives, to students, and parents, and to other participants vary greatly across public and private nonprofit institutions" (p. 24). Hence, as is the case throughout the book, attention will be given to variations across institutional type and forms of institutional control.

Reed (2017) states, "The underlying assumption of shared governance is that everyone agrees about who is sharing" (Reed, 2017, p. 428). However, in including *stakeholders* as an important element of the framing for this chapter, we are mindful of Fish's (2007) caution regarding this postulation when it comes to shared governance in higher education. He rightly points out that the list of commonly understood stakeholders, those "who are (or might be) affected by an action taken by an organization or group" (Wikipedia Encyclopedia as cited by Fish, 2007), is long, and Fish goes on to point out that the creation of such a list invites claims from others who have been omitted but feel they have a right to inclusion. This concern is not a new one. As Barrett and Quarless (2017) point out, "the role of constituents in the formation of policy and operation of a college has been part of the academic landscape since the operation of the Academy, in both ancient Greece and Europe" (p. 43). Fish (2007) argues that it is better in discussing shared governance to focus on what it is that we do on a particular campus as opposed to focus on who it is that might be affected in some way by our efforts. While encouraging readers to give serious consideration to Fish's thoughtful and principled analysis, the purpose of this chapter is helping professionals in higher education (and student affairs professionals in particular) become familiar with both the platforms and the participants of shared governance and therefore lends itself to discussion of the interconnected structures and stakeholders with whom those professionals may come in contact.

The common structures of shared governance are addressed in this chapter from those with the broadest span of interest and authority to those with the narrowest. It is not our intention in doing so to reinforce a hierarchical perspective on shared governance as each of these structures has an important role to play. As each of the various structures is described and discussed, the stakeholders whose interests are represented by the structures are identified.

Governing Boards

Lingenfelter (2004) comments, "The relationship between higher education and the state has become essential, but it has never been easy. . . . Both history and contemporary practice affirm the deep interdependence between higher education and the state" (p. 47). Higher education is, after all, a state function (noting exceptions such as tribally controlled colleges or military service academies), and governing boards are the mechanism through which states typically carry out this function.

In as much as they are public governing entities, the stakeholders whose interests are ostensibly served by statewide higher education governing boards are the people of the state. It is for this reason that these boards are predominately populated by persons with no formal role at a higher education institution in that state, though the governing boards sometimes include a member representing faculty or student interests.

The scope of authority and specific responsibilities of these governing boards vary from state to state. Bracco, Richardson, Callan, and Finney (1999) offer a taxonomy of state governing boards which identifies three broad types. They are:

1. Consolidated governing boards have responsibility for operational activities, line authority over higher education institutions. They are a centralized mode of state-university governance.
2. Coordinating boards facilitate communications and coordinate higher education initiative and research across the state's higher education institutions.
3. State planning boards have limited statewide coordinating authority and are largely advisory in their function.

Some states have a single unified governing board with authority or responsibility for all institutions in the state. Others have one board for four-year institutions and another for two-year institutions.

The ways in which state governing boards engage in shared governance varies by the type of board is at hand. Many within higher education are concerned by what they perceive to be increasing intrusion by these boards into aspects of campus decision-making such as curriculum, considerations of tenure or other aspects of academic working conditions, enrollment policies, or student life issues which are seen as reserved for control by various campus-based structures in a traditional understanding of shared governance (Carnegie Commission on Higher Education, 1973; Davis, 2006). It is worth noting that the *Statement on Government of Colleges and Universities* (AAUP, 1967) makes only oblique references with regard to the role of statewide governing boards, and those comments can fairly be characterized as something other than sanguine. Whatever the type and whatever the role, "The challenges of decision making, as well as communicating, organizing, and disagreeing within a shared governance model within an individual institution are many. Within large statewide systems of higher education, these challenges are exponentially increased" (Cramer & Mozlin, 2017, p. 89).

Direct interactions between a given institution or a higher education system within a state and governing board members typically take place only at the most senior administrative or faculty levels. Senior student affairs professionals could be involved in helping develop or review presentations for a board. They are also likely to be involved at the institutional cabinet level in conversations related to presenting institutional concerns or priorities to the board or as part of a system- or state-wide working group taking part in similar conversations. It is rare, though not unheard of, that a senior student affairs officer might be called upon to provide a report directly to the board on a particular topic. Higher education professionals at the early and mid-points of their careers are not likely to have direct contact with members of governing boards. They may, however, be called upon to help produce reports which will inform and influence board deliberations or to help someone prepare for a presentation to the board.

Direct contact between individual institutions or systems is an integral part of the governing process. Such contacts are likely to be between senior- or mid-level leadership and board staff and are typically related to sharing information for board consideration or efforts on the part of the institution or system to have an early influence on the articulation or direction of potential board policy.

Indirect contact between an institution or a system and the governing board is also important. State legislators, leaders of business or local government, and other persons of influence are often asked by higher education to reach out to governing board members to help influence particular considerations. Like direct contact, these efforts are typically the province of senior administrative or faculty leadership of the institution or system.

Boards of Trustees

While the terminology varies to include boards of trustees (used throughout this chapter for sake of simplicity), boards of regents, boards of visitors, boards of overseers, and more (Worth, 2008), lay boards have been and continue to be a defining characteristic of American higher education. "Throughout much of the history of American colleges and universities . . . faculty exercised little influence over the formulation of educational policies or other aspects of decision making. Instead, American institutions of higher learning very early on came to be distinguished from European universities by the development of strong external governing boards and presidents" (Gerber, 2014, p. 3). Like the statewide governing boards, boards of trustees at both private (used here and throughout the chapter to refer to independent not-for-profit institutions) and public institutions serve as stewards of the public's interests in higher education. Governance structures at private for-profit institutions vary depending on the underlying corporate structure and articles of incorporation for a given institution, and the specifics of those variations are beyond the scope of this chapter.

The board of trustees "possesses fundamental legal authority over the university. The authority of the governing board is vested in it by the state wherein the school resides or, particularly in the case of older, private institutions, by legally binding royal or colonial charters" (Pusser & Loss, 2018, ¶5). Boards of trustees can be for a single campus, a given campus in a multicampus university, or for a statewide system (Worth, 2008). Their formal responsibilities "are significant even as they are few in number. They include preservation of the university charter; institutional performance evaluations; fundraising; liaison with external agencies and political bodies; budget approval; oversight of campus policies and investment strategies; and perhaps, most important, hiring and evaluating the ongoing performance of the university president" (Pusser & Loss, 2018, ¶8).

With regard to the role of boards of trustees in shared governance, the *Statement on Government of Colleges and Universities* (AAUP, 1967) states:

> The board helps relate the institution to its chief community: for example, the community college to serve the educational needs of a defined population area or group, the church-controlled college to be cognizant of the announced position of its denomination, and the comprehensive university to discharge the many duties and to accept the appropriate new challenges which are its concern at the several levels of higher education. The governing board of an institution of higher education in the United States operates, with few exceptions, as the final institutional authority. . . . The governing board of an institution of higher education, while maintaining a general overview, entrusts the conduct of administration to the administrative officers—the president and the deans—and the conduct of teaching and research to the faculty. The board should undertake appropriate self-limitation. . . . The board plays a central role in relating the likely needs of the future to predictable resources; it has the responsibility for husbanding the endowment; it is responsible for obtaining needed capital and operating funds; and in the broadest sense of the term it should pay attention to personnel policy. In order to fulfill these duties, the board should be aided by, and may insist upon, the development of long-range planning by the administration and faculty. (AAUP, 1967, ¶22–26)

Most boards of trustees at private institutions are self-perpetuating, meaning that the board is responsible for selecting its own members (Worth, 2008). Some private institutions have two boards. Harvard is an example of such an institution. Their President and Fellows of Harvard College (or Harvard Corporation) serves as an executive board which handles finances and education policy, and their Board of Overseers (with members selected by the alumni) advises the president and approves some of their actions such as the appointment of key administrative and academic personnel (Worth, 2008). At public institutions, members of the boards of trustees are typically appointed by the state's governor with approval by the state's legislature. Some states do have elected trustees for their public institutions (Worth, 2008).

Some boards of trustees, both public and private, have presidents of institutions as ex officio members. A relatively small proportion of boards of trustees also have ex officio seats reserved for various constituencies such as alumni, faculty, or students. Marting (2003) found that 10.7 percent of private and 3.4 percent of public boards have faculty members; 9.3 percent of privates and 20.5 percent of publics have students as members.

The patterns of interaction between community members at a higher education institution and members of the board of trustees for that institution are very similar to the interactions between community members and members of the governing boards discussed earlier. Senior leadership is most likely to interact directly with board members. Mid-level administrative leadership may interact directly with board staff on occasion, and early-career professionals are typically limited to indirect contact. Boards of trustees are commonly organized into committees, and it is fairly typical for there to be a committee assigned with oversight of matters directly related to the student experience. It is with trustees serving on this committee that student affairs professionals at all levels are most likely to have direct or indirect contact.

Administration

Conversations amongst people involved in higher education about campus matters, including those related to shared governance, are sometimes framed with reference to students, staff, faculty, and administration where the last group may be labeled as the dreaded *them.* As used in such conversations, administration may refer to a broad and indeterminate swath of institutional employees including the most senior level offices as well as their second- and third-level associates. The growth in the administrative class within university organizational structures is the subject of a good deal of debate, much of which is outside the scope of this book. Here it will suffice to note, "the rapid expansion of college administration that has occurred over the last century and more was not only a result of the increasing size and complexity of American institutions of higher education; it was also at least in part a product of the desire on many faculty members to avoid administrative responsibilities for both the formulation and implementation of policies" (Gerber, 2014, p. 8). It is helpful to keep in mind that one of the tendencies of any profession is to lay claim to expertise and, through that claim, to control. Recalling Wilensky's

(1964) observation about the push by fields to become seen as professional and the perceptions some in higher education about the growing number of administrative professionals, it is not surprising that tensions can arise about who has expertise, in what areas is that expertise, and how should that be accounted for (if at all) in matters of shared governance (Etzioni, 1964).

Practically speaking, the president of an institution is the administration in as much as the board of trustees delegate authority and responsibility to that office which in turn delegates both back out to other executive officers and their divisions. Pusser and Loss (2018) explain, "The liaison between a postsecondary institution and its governing board is the highest ranking executive officer, a president or chancellor. The president provides overall leadership to the institution and presides over its academic and administrative bureaus" (¶10).

It is not unexpected to find extended commentary in the *Statement on Government of Colleges and Universities* (AAUP, 1967) on the role of the president in shared governance.

> The president shares responsibility for the definition and attainment of goals, for administrative action, and for operating the communications system that links the components of the academic community. The president represents the institution to its many publics. The president's leadership role is supported by delegated authority from the board and faculty. . . . The president must at times, with or without support, infuse new life into a department; relatedly, the president may at times be required, working within the concept of tenure, to solve problems of obsolescence. The president will necessarily utilize the judgments of the faculty but may also, in the interest of academic standards, seek outside evaluations by scholars of acknowledged competence. It is the duty of the president to see to it that the standards and procedures in operational use within the college or university conform to the policy established by the governing board and to the standards of sound academic practice. It is also incumbent on the president to ensure that faculty views, including dissenting views, are presented to the board in those areas and on those issues where responsibilities are shared. Similarly, the faculty should be informed of the views of the board and the administration on like issues. The president is largely responsible for the maintenance of existing institutional resources and the creation of new resources; has ultimate managerial responsibility for a large area of nonacademic

activities; is responsible for public understanding; and by the nature of the office is the chief person who speaks for the institution. (AAUP, 1967, ¶27–31)

The question of which stakeholders are represented by the administration in shared governance is an interesting one to consider. Senior administrators and their key staff may consider themselves as representing the institution as a whole or the board of trustees. The vice presidents might also see themselves as advocating for the interests of the president or of their division. They might also understand their efforts as being on behalf of a constituency organized or served in their division (students in the case of student affairs, faculty in the case of academic affairs, staff in the case of business affairs, or alumni and donors in the case of development). Of course, they may be undertaking this advocacy as part of a collaborative political effort and so at some level serving the stakeholders across that particular collaborative effort (there will be more on politics and partnership in Chapter Four).

The vice president for student affairs (senior student affairs officer), dean of students, and other associate or assistant vice presidents, who are typically counted as administration in campus parlance, almost certainly interact with one another as well as with their peers in other divisions of the institution as well as with leadership of the various senates in the course of exploring and addressing issues through a shared governance process.

Senates

We now turn our attention to a group of structures which serve particular constituencies within higher education institutions or systems. As is the case with boards of trustees, these structures go by a variety of names—associations, councils, governments, or senates being among some of the common ones. The term *senate* will be used in discussing these groups throughout this chapter.

Faculty, student, and staff senates are common throughout American higher education. An essential defining characteristic of these groups with regard to their role in shared governance is that the vast majority of their members are elected by the stakeholders they serve. "Importantly, faculty senates, staff senates, and student government associations provide the means through which consensus building can take place. A shared governance body represents a collective voice, without which a cacophony of loud individual voices can emerge predominant" (Dudley-Eshbach, 2011, ¶2).

Faculty Senates

As noted in Chapter One, one of the consequences of the professionalization of the faculty in U.S. higher education was increased expectations on their part for academic freedom and for a significant role in governance.

> Such claims for a greater role in academic decision making had their first major impact on the ability of faculty members to assert control over what went on in their own classrooms. This was followed by a general recognition throughout American higher education of the faculty's claim to primary responsibility for determining the curriculum and the graduation requirements. . . . The development of a significant faculty role in governance was a slow and uneven process. At no time did American faculty members come to enjoy anything close to full control of the institutions in which they taught and did research. (Gerber, 2014, p. 5)

Another important consequence of faculty professionalization was the development of discipline-based departments (Gerber, 2014). Today faculty control over curricular matters as well as their significant role in matters of educational policy, hiring of faculty, and other matters of personnel, policy, and finance are based at the department level and then aggregate to the level of college or school and finally at the institutional level. Members of the faculty senate are elected at the department level; executive officers of the faculty senate are elected on an at-large basis by the eligible faculty.

Pusser and Loss (2018) note, "The formal governing body of the faculty at the institutional level is the academic senate, a body generally comprised of tenured and tenure-track faculty from the various disciplines and professional schools. The faculty senate and its attendant committees provide elected faculty liaisons to the university board and president. A primary function of the senate is to represent the voice of the faculty in matters of university governance" (¶13). The Statement on Government of Colleges and Universities (AAUP, 1967) affirms:

> The faculty has primary responsibility for such fundamental areas as curriculum, subject matter and methods of instruction, research, faculty status, and those aspects of student life which relate to the educational process [footnote on role in admissions added in 2002 With regard to student admissions, the faculty should have a meaningful role in establishing institutional policies, including the setting of standards for admission, and should be afforded opportunity for oversight of the entire admissions process]. . . . The faculty sets the requirements for the degrees offered in course, determines when the requirements have been met, and authorizes the president and board to grant the degrees thus achieved. Faculty status and related matters are primarily a faculty responsibility; this area includes appointments, reappointments, decisions not to reappoint, promotions, the granting of tenure, and dismissal. . . . Determinations in these matters should first be by faculty action through established procedures, reviewed by the chief academic officers with the concurrence of the board. The governing board and president should, on questions of faculty status, as in other matters where the faculty has primary responsibility, concur with the faculty judgment except in rare instances and for compelling reasons which should be stated in detail. . . . The chair or head of a department, who serves as the chief representative of the department within an institution, should be selected either by departmental election or by appointment following consultation with members of the department and of related departments; appointments should normally be in conformity with department members' judgment. . . . Agencies for faculty participation in the government of the college or university should be established at each level where faculty responsibility is present. . . . Faculty representatives should be selected by the faculty according to procedures determined by the faculty. (AAUP, 1967, ¶32–38)

While there are changes afoot in the composition of faculty senates across the nation, it is still not the case that all faculty members are represented in these structures. Distinctions have been made on the basis of rank and tenure-status on eligibility to be a senate member or to vote on certain issues. "Involvement in research is thus often cited creating the expertise that is required for informed participation in many aspects of academic decision making. Consequently, some have raised doubts as to whether faculty members whose academic responsibilities do not include research ought to be given a substantial role in the shaping of their institution's educational policies. In particular, this has been an issue in the community college sector" (Gerber, 2014, p. 7).

Some faculty senates do provide for ex officio membership for non-faculty community members. Where they exist in faculty senates, ex officio spots (sometimes with voting privileges and sometimes without) are commonly held for senior administrative and academic leadership or for leaders of student or staff senates (Miller, Smith, & Nadler, 2016).

Like boards of trustees, it is common practice for one committee in faculty senates to be charged with deliberation in matters related to student life. This may include student conduct policies, enrollment management issues, and other matters of student welfare or the student experience.

It is not surprising given the local focus of the faculty governance groups, the topics of concern to them, or the relative frequency of their meetings at both the department and institutional levels (when compared with either statewide governing boards or board of trustees) that student affairs professionals at all career levels are likely to directly interact with their members in the course of shared governance matters. In some instances, student affairs professionals may be invited to serve as members of faculty sub-committees or working groups. They may also be invited to take part in particular meetings or to share information or perspectives for consideration by the faculty group. Student affairs professionals may also indirectly interact with faculty shared governance groups through helping to identify students to participate or through supporting those students in their participation.

Student Senates

Cowley (1980) suggests student governance entities can be understood as central or peripheral (the term peripheral seems marginalizing of both the issues and the student effort involved). The former address broad student affairs issues; the later deals with specific subunits (campus housing or athletics, for example). The central student structure of student senates will be addressed in this section, and the other student structures will be addressed later in this chapter.

Student senates have been a part of American higher education since the late eighteenth century (Hall, 1962; Klopf, 1960), but Pusser and Loss (2018) observes "historically students have not had a significant role in the organizational structure or governance of colleges and universities" (¶21). While not in complete agreement with that assessment, there is little doubt that the degree to which student governments play a role in shared governance varies across higher education in the United States with institutional culture and history, institutional mission, type of institutional control (public or private), demographics of students enrolled, and contemporary issues at hand all accounting for some part of that variance.

The *Statement on Government of Colleges and Universities* (AAUP, 1967) encourages facilitating student participation in student governance. It states:

> When students in American colleges and universities desire to participate responsibly in the government of the institution they attend, their wish should be recognized as a claim to opportunity both for educational experience and for involvement in the affairs of their college or university. Ways should be found to permit significant student participation within the limits of attainable effectiveness. The obstacles to such participation are large and should not be minimized: inexperience, untested capacity, a transitory status which means that present action does not carry with it subsequent responsibility, and the inescapable fact that the other components of the institution are in a position of judgment over the students. It is important to recognize that student needs are strongly related to educational experience, both formal and informal. (AAUP, 1967, ¶40)

Here again there is no standard terminology for the central student governance structures. Common names include association, government, senate, and union. Where an institution enrolls both undergraduate and graduate or professional degree students then it is likely that there will be separate senates serving the two groups. The structure of student senates may include an executive, legislative, and judicial branch. Student senates are also sometimes home to campus programming boards, a practice more common at smaller campuses. Stand-alone programming boards are more likely at larger campuses.

Executive officers are elected on an at-large basis. Senators are typically selected to represent a specific constituency such residence halls (or commuting students), Greek units, student organizations, degree level (undergraduate or graduate and professional program), school or college, or at-large. Selection typically takes place through election, though some student senates are self-selecting. Judicial branch members are usually selected through nomination by the executive branch with approval by the legislative branch.

It should come as no surprise that student affairs professionals at all levels have a high degree of interaction with student senates. Those interactions may take the form of direct advising of the senate, participation in discussion of matters before the senate, or review of funding requests where student affairs programs and services are supported in part or in whole through student fees allocated by the senate. Student affairs professionals may also have indirect involvement with student senates through their role in advising student organizations which may be seeking recognition, requesting funding, or bringing forward a concern for consideration.

Staff Senates

It is arguably the case that no stakeholder group has received less attention in the literature on shared governance in higher education than the general staff (as distinct from the broader term *employees* which would include senior administration and faculty with graduate assistants and both undergraduate and graduate students working at an institution). Indeed, staff go unmentioned in the *Statement on Government of Colleges and Universities* (AAUP, 1967).

This is not to say that staff are absent from the contemporary practice of shared governance in American higher education. Staff senates (also referred to as councils) offer advice on and give voice to a variety of concerns related to conditions and terms of employment and typically provide representation on certain university committees and as a part of the selection of senior administrative leadership, though their reach infrequently extends beyond those issues.

Smaller institutions may have only one staff senate with spaces reserved for members representing the various employment categories (for example, administrative professionals, clerical/technical, and service workers). Larger campuses may have a senate for each of the employment categories. Executive officers for the staff senates are either elected or selected from among the elected senate members.

Because the focus of staff senates is largely on conditions of employment and the working environment at an institution there is not often a reason for student affairs professionals to interact directly with them on matters before the body. However, student affairs members can and do serve as members of the staff senate for their respective employment category.

Unions

The role of unions in shared governance is a matter of some discussion in the literature of higher education (see the opposing viewpoints expressed by Burbules (2013) and Benjamin (2013) for example). While not a governance structure *per se,* they may have an impact on shared governance at institutions through the terms of collective bargaining agreements between local union branches and institutions of higher education.

Faculty unionization began in the late 1960s and early 1970s at a time when higher education in the United States was coming under economic pressure (Gerber, 2014). The unionization of faculty is more common at institutions which are less research intensive and which may be seen by some as less prestigious and where the tradition of shared governance is less fully developed and pronounced (Gerber, 2014). Writing about the role of unionization in shared governance at Historically Black Colleges and Universities, Davenport (2015) states, "collective bargaining is the ultimate shared governance tool. . . . The contracts negotiated through the collective bargaining process acknowledge and legitimize shared governance, and convey power to faculty unions" (p. 46). The majority of public community colleges in American have unionized faculty (Kater & Levin, 2004).

"For community colleges, shared governance reemerged in the literature in the late 1980s on the heels of the California Assembly's Bill 1725, which codified the legal authority for higher education in the state between a state board and local governing boards. The bill also increased the governance activities and responsibilities of faculty through academic senates. State legislation required management to allow faculty to participate in governance" (Kater & Levin, 2004, p. 5). Using this legislation as a springboard for their work, Kater and Levin (2004) studied the labor contracts for 301 public, unionized community colleges to explore the ways in which shared governance was addressed, if at all, in those agreements. They found that "the collective-bargaining process has allowed for the development of many areas of shared or participatory decision-making and institutional action" (Kater & Levin, 2004, p. 2) and noted, "this study indicates that centralization of decision-making through collective bargaining does not limit faculty participation in governance. Bargaining as a political form of governance has enshrined faculty rights and responsibilities in collective agreements that are binding on both the faculty and management" (Kater & Levin, 2004, p. 19).

It is not only faculty that may be unionized labor in higher education. Another shared governance structural development from the 1960s and 70s was the development of graduate student unions (Bray, 2006). More recently, a series of rulings by the National Labor Relations Board (NLRB) permit the unionization of both undergraduate and graduate student employees at private institutions (Hong, 2017). There has also been an initial administrative ruling by the NLRB that permitted student-athletes at a private institution to explore unionization, though that ruling was subsequently overturned upon a full NLRB panel review (Strauss, 2015). Collective bargaining by employees at public higher education institutions is governed by state law, and graduate student unions are more common at public institutions. Little, if any, attention is given in the literature to the relationship between shared governance and the unionization of these other employee groups in American higher education, but it is not unreasonable to assume that the negotiated labor agreements into which they enter would be the mechanism through which shared governance could be addressed.

Other Student Governance Groups

Student senates are not the only shared governance group for which students are the primary stakeholders. As noted earlier, there may be any number of student organizations which offer input or hold responsibility for specific programs and services. Common examples include student governance groups for Greek life, residential life, or the student-athlete experience. There are two essential requirements in order for any of these groups to be thought of as governance structures. First, they must be recognized as such by the institution with a clear understanding of the elements of institutional life for which the group's input will be seen as appropriate and any delegated authority which will reside with the group. Second, membership must either be elected or self-selecting without requirement of approval from some other source.

Student affairs professionals at all career levels are likely to interact directly with these student governance groups either as advisors or as participants in the institutional consideration of issues of interest to the student governance group. Student affairs professionals may also be indirectly involved with these groups through providing developmental programs related to ethics, inclusion, or leadership.

Advisory Councils

Advisory councils are another structure in shared governance. These councils are found at the academic and administrative unit level as well as at the school or college and institutional level. "The responsibilities of advisory board members are quite different from a board of directors or board of trustees in that the advisory board exercises no authority–fiduciary, policy-making, legal, or otherwise–over the department or college" (Nagai & Nehls, 2013, pp. 3–4). While they may have no authority, they may have influence. Boards of trustees also occasionally delegate particular responsibilities to advisory councils. These usually relate to limited affiliated programs such as a college radio station (Worth, 2008).

In a study of nearly 500 higher education institutions, Worth (2008) found that one-third had institution-wide advisory councils and 73 percent of deans at private institutions and 78 percent of deans at public institutions had one or more advisory councils associated with their school or college. There is, however, a dearth of literature on advisory councils despite their prevalence in practice (Nagai & Nehls, 2013).

Members of advisory councils are typically appointed by the academic or administrative leader for the department or unit with which the council is affiliated. The most common constituencies from which members are drawn are alumni, donors and prospects other than alumni, corporate executives, and community leaders (Worth, 2008). Responsibilities for advisory council members may include being ambassadors and advocates, sharing advice, promoting visibility and image, sharing nonfinancial resources, participating in meetings and programs, and light fundraising (Worth, 2008). Nagai and Nehls (2013) report non-alumni volunteers' reasons for agreeing to serve include wanting to make a difference, having commitment to education, and fulfilling expectations of employer. Volunteers also interested in interacting with students and connecting with faculty.

Ellingson, Elbert, and Moser (2010) studied advisory councils associated with business schools and identified a number of resources that a council has to offer. These resources, which seem like they would be true of advising councils for all academic and administrative units, include "assisting in strategic planning and mission development, providing counsel on administrative issues, financial support and fundraising, networking and relations with external constituencies such as alumni and the community, student internships and placement, curriculum and program assessment, speakers for classes or events, and faculty issues and resources" (Ellingson, Elbert, & Moser, 2010, p. 1).

While it may seem that having volunteers to share their advice, experiences, and insights seems like a straightforward positive proposition, there are some challenges to fully engaging the benefits of an advisory council. It "requires times and effort that may not be valued by the institution . . . faculty may oppose or resist the council's recommendations . . . [council] may be underutilized for several reasons, including not clearly identifying the role of the council . . . or spending too much meeting time on college updates and progress reports and not allowing enough time for council members to discuss issues and provide insights or share the experience" (Ellingson, Elbert, & Moser, 2010, p. 2).

The stakeholders reflected in advisory council are external and vary based on the specific focus of a given council. Examples of stakeholders include business interests, community leadership, or parents.

Senior student affairs officers may interact with advisory councils for the institution. They, and other student affairs colleagues, could also engaged with advisory councils for the student affairs division or for student affairs units.

Alumni Associations

Alumni "have had a voice in institutional affairs for centuries" (Cowley, 1980, p. 130). Early examples by American education institutions to engage their alumni include the role of alumni on Harvard's Board of Overseers (Crowley, 1980), Yale's notes on its graduate, or the organization of alumni at Williams College and Princeton University (Worth, 2008).

Alumni organizations are commonly called alumni associations in contemporary practice. These associations serve to help alumni stay connected with their alma mater and with one another. They assist in gathering financial and non-financial resources for the institution, helping with recruitment, and raising visibility and image. Alumni associations can also serve as a valuable sounding board for considerations of institutional policy, practice, and strategic priorities. Institutions may have one overarching alumni association with a variety of alumni groups representing academic colleges, states or regions, student interests (student-athletes or student leaders for example), or identity affiliation (such as African Americans or persons who identify as LGBTQ).

Alumni boards provide oversight for the overarching alumni association and coordination of the efforts of the alumni groups. Like advisory councils, alumni boards have no authority in shared governance but may have influence. Some institutions involve their alumni boards in the nomination to fill alumni spaces on the board of trustees. It goes without question that alumni are the stakeholders whose interest are at the forefront of alumni association boards in matters of shared governance.

Alumni boards may be independent, dependent, or interrelated with respect to staffing and support (Worth, 2008). Membership for alumni boards is frequently self-selecting. with an effort being made to include representation from across various alumni constituencies.

Student affairs professionals may engage with alumni associations in either their work roles or as alumni of the institution. Connecting students with alumni through mentoring or internship programs, helping to support the development of identity affiliated alumni groups or student interest alumni groups, and calling on alumni to help support various student affairs programs and services are among the ways in which student affairs professionals interact through their work roles with alumni associations and boards.

Many institutions also have an affiliated foundation which is a separate 501(c)(3) corporation. Foundations serve to raise money and hold assets for a university. Like alumni associations, these foundations may be independent, dependent, or interrelated with respect to staffing and support (Worth, 2008). Foundation board members may be alumni, but they are also likely to be non-alumni business or civic leaders. These foundations and their boards are not a part a shared governance structure in that they serve purely a service function for their host institution and have neither responsibility nor influence on institutional policy or practice (though some members of a foundation board may also be members of other shared governance structures for the institution).

Other Governance Groups

This chapter has offered a discussion of the most common shared governance structures in higher education, but there are other groups which may play a role in the governance of institutions. In as much as higher education institutions and the higher education system in America are open, consideration should be given to groups external to higher education institutions which may have an influence on their governance. Associations are a large broad category of external groups. Cowley (1980) lists 15 types of associations which may have influence. The list includes (with examples of each type listed in parenthesis):

1. Accrediting bodies (regional and professional)
2. Subject-matter societies (American Chemical Society)
3. Broad subject-area councils (American Council of Learned Societies)
4. Organization of analogous institutions (Association of American Universities)
5. Societies of administrators (NACUBO)
6. Organizations of college and university trustees (AGB)
7. Fund-raising agencies (Council for Financial Aid to Education)
8. Agencies performing various services for college and universities (ETS)
9. Subdivisions of religious denominations (Association of Jesuit Colleges and Universities)
10. Groups devoted to furthering various education enterprises (Institute of International Educators)
11. Councils and associations concerned with higher education in general either nationally or regionally (American Association for Higher Education)
12. International bodies (UNESCO)

13. Groups devoted to the advancement and preservation of faculty prerogatives (AAUP)
14. Honorary fraternities (Phi Betta Kappa)
15. Honorific academies (American Academy of Arts and Sciences)

Institutional Committees and Task Forces

Some readers are by now asking what about university committees and task forces? These are the structures through which a great deal of business gets done at higher education institutions across the land, but are they shared governance groups? The answer, like the answer to many good questions, is that it depends. Asking two important questions can help clarify the answer. First, are these committees and task forces duplicative of elements of extant shared governance structures so that they essentially are an alternative workaround to those elements? Second, how are the members of these committees and task forces selected? Are they elected by the stakeholders or appointed by elected representatives of the stakeholders, or are they appointment by some entity other than the stakeholders they are to represent? Committees and task forces can be helpful means through which to transact either one-time, episodic, or ongoing conversations. However, attention should be given to whether these conversations might be better suited to regular shared governance channels (Bahls, 2014; Quarless & Barrett, 2017). Doing otherwise might lead to the results of the discussions being seen as illegitimate and competing advice or decisions being put forth by the recognized shared governance entity.

Proposing a New Course of Study at New Pacific University

New Pacific University (NPU) is an elite, highly selective, research intensive private university located on the California coastline. It prides itself on academic rigor and on its nationally and internationally recognized faculty. Like many colleges across the country, NPU has seen important and welcome changes in the diversity of its student body over the past 20 years. Those changes have resulted in the need for some changes in the programs and services offered at the institution, but there has not been any significant change in curricular offerings. Over the past several years, however, Asian American and Pacific Islander students have begun asking for more opportunities for courses related to their cultures and identities. A very small number of faculty have made some changes in existing courses in response to student comments. However, no new courses, minors, or majors have been added, and there are currently no discussions under way regarding any such changes. Frustrated by what they perceive as institutional indifference to their interests and identifies, an ad hoc coalition of the Asian American and Pacific Islander student organizations at NPU forms. They bring their concerns to NPU's Dean of Students who listens empathetically and informs them about how curricular decisions are made at NPU. He encourages them to identify an academic program or two in which there might be faculty allies who would work with them to develop proposals to add several courses. Later, assuming the courses are approved and then supported through student enrollment, conversations can begin with faculty allies about the possibility of crafting a minor or major that could be routed through the shared governance process for consideration and hopefully approval. The students appreciate the time the Dean spends with them, but they are unhappy about what sounds like a long and protracted process to achieve what seems to them to be an obvious rightful outcome. They begin discussing other ways to pursue their goal and decide to request meetings with the provost, president, and chair of the board of trustees. They also reach out through social media to alumni, parents, and Asian American and Pacific Islander advocacy organizations through social media. The students' efforts being to receive media attention, and there is talk of students taking direct symbolic non-violent action in the form of blocking campus buildings or walking out of classes which are not inclusive of Asian American or Pacific Islander concerns.

Things are escalating quickly. What do you think the provost, president, and chair of the board of trustees should do? Are there other leaders who might step forward? If so, how?

PUTTING THEM TOGETHER THE RIGHT WAY

Any discussion such as the one shared in this chapter ought to include recognition that "the ways in which institutions should be governed, and the roles of various parties in this process, are an enduring and often contested area of both practice and inquiry. The question of participation has particular relevance for organisations where key groups of members occupy dependent, vulnerable, or low-status roles" (Lizio & Wilson 2009, p. 69). Miller, Smith, and Nadler (2016) add, "Shared governance in higher education has an historical foundation that includes representation by students, faculty, trustees, and increasingly, staff members. Each of these constituents engage to various extents, in offering advice to college leaders, reactions to proposals, and in many cases, offering resolutions or actions for programs or policies. Through an evolution of the structure and administration, each of these constituents has also had to advocate for their rights to be engage in campus decision-making, with some success and some failures" (p. 22).

How then to identify the most satisficing (Simon, 1956) shared governance scaffolding for a particular institution? Austin and Jones (2016) encourage looking to the institutional mission. They state, "governance structures should be designed to help a university to accomplish its mission. It is generally believed that the better the governance arrangement, the greater the benefits to be derived from it and the greater the chance of the organization achieving its mission" (p. 8). Given the number and diversity of interests and roles involved, it is critically important in whatever shape the scaffolding takes to clearly define and maintain the roles and responsibilities of the various structures and stakeholders (Marting, 2003; Worth, 2008).

REFLECTION QUESTIONS

1. Who are the shared governance shareholders with whom you might interact in the course of the role you play at your higher education institution?
2. What are the shared governance structures with which you might interact in the course of the role you play at your higher education institution?

3. How are the lists of structures and shareholders shaped by the type of institution (including type of control) with which you are affiliated?
4. What are the practices, policies, or documents at your institution which help clearly identify and define the role of various structures and stakeholders in shared governance?
5. What, if any, practices, policies, or documents at your institution serve to blur roles and responsibilities of various structures and stakeholders in shared governance?
6. How might the case study discussed in this chapter play out at your institution with respect to shared governance? Who would be the interested stakeholders? What governance structures might serve to include those stakeholders in the deliberations?

Chapter 3

HOW TO HELP FOSTER AND STRENGTHEN SHARED GOVERNANCE

Governance in colleges and universities is customarily viewed as the domain of executive offers, boards of trustees, and faculty senates. In the literature, student affairs divisions are not characteristically connected to governance; yet these divisions are part of colleges and universities; student affairs divisions are both participants in the organization and subject to governance processes and outcomes.

Levin (2009, p. 45)

Equipped with a general understanding of shared governance and of the stakeholders and structures party to it, we turn our attention to the ways in which we in higher education (and particularly in student affairs professional positions) can help foster and strengthen shared governance. It can be argued that seeking to understand shared governance better through the information in Chapters One and Two were the first steps in that journey, albeit fairly tentative steps. How can we take more bold strides? It is the aim of this chapter to offer advice and suggestions for action in just that endeavor.

Next Steps at Great Golden Plains Community College

Great Golden Plains Community College (GGPCC) is a relatively stable institution located in a rural area of a northern plains state, and most of its students are enrolled in technical training programs related to servicing the agricultural, energy, and transportation industries which drive a great deal of the local economy. Much of their academic and co-curricular programming reflects practices that in place for some time, and there are no major change initiatives afoot. The senior administrative and faculty leadership have all be in place for a number of years. Their relationship is amenable and can best be characterized as keeping out of one another's way on most things. However, a recent accreditation visit and report included some note of dissatisfaction among business and civic leaders that the institution is not playing a role in innovation and advancement in the region. The accreditation report went on to question whether or not the stasis and comfortable go-along-to-get-along climate of shared governance is serving the institution and its community as well as it might. The state governing board for community colleges has highlighted these aspects of the report and has asked that the institution consider ways of revitalizing its shared governance with particular attention given to bringing new voices into the various processes. The good news is that there is no crisis of confidence at hand, but there is a genuine desire on the part of the board to have GGPCC seen as more than just an adequate support for the region and a belief on their part that innovation can and should come about through taking advantage of the opportunities presented for strategic planning and action through shared governance. The president of GGPCC has asked all cabinet members to develop plans for encouraging broad participation in shared governance and to be certain that those plans address reaching out to all members of the community. As the vice president for student affairs begins to ponder how to follow through on this assignment for their division, what are the specific ways in which they can make a difference? Who are the folks to whom the division ought to reach out, and how can that effort lead to great involvement absent a particular issue driving the discussion? What are the knowledge and skill sets within the division that student affairs staff can draw on in pursuing the work which needs to be done?

ARTICULATING GOALS FOR SHARED GOVERNANCE

A helpful step in strengthening shared governance on campus is to develop a community understanding of what the institution's goals are with respect to shared governance. Put another way, what will good shared governance look like on campus?

Venable and Gardiner (1988) list six characteristics which distinguish genuine shared governance. The six are:

1. Climate of trust
2. Information sharing
3. Meaningful participation
4. Collective decision making
5. Protecting divergent views
6. Redefining roles

Those interested in a more detailed example might consider nine suggestions for good the good practice shared governance offered by Bejou and Bejou (2016). They are:

1. Governance is truly shared, especially between administration and faculty–that is, governance occurs in a participatory and collaborative fashion in which (a) differences in the weight of each voice should be determined by reference to the responsibility of each component for the particular matter at hand, (b) all recognize the existence of timeframes imposed by state and federal agencies, and (c) ongoing consultation and communication among all affected components is guaranteed at all times (i.e., no components will ever be left out of decision-making procedures).
2. Governance is transparent and straightforward–that is, all persons and components of the university understand how things are supposed to work, who does what and why, who has authority to do what, what the proper channels and procedures are, and so on.
3. Governance follows a consistent planning and evaluation model (short-, medium-, long-term planning is consistently followed by evaluation and encourages participation by competent members of the university community).

4. Governance works in a timely and efficient way (i.e., processes are as simple and straightforward as possible—task and responsibility oriented) and is responsive to the needs of all university constituencies.
5. Governance is stable and successful enough to withstand undue outside interference, weaknesses in personal performance/leadership, and personal conflicts.
6. Governance recognizes the duties and responsibilities that are assigned by the board and/or the president to the senior officers, deans, directors, and department chairs.
7. The governance structure supports a university culture that is based on a common mission and strategic goals that are founded on the members of the university community (which includes attracting highly competent and dedicated people to specific tasks and duties).
8. The governance structure allows for resource allocation that stresses the overall importance of advancing academic efforts and education.
9. Governance is flexible and responsive enough to meet standards befitting an academic institution that pursues. (Bejou & Bejou, 2016, p. 58)

One can, and the authors argue, should adopt a more inclusive list of partners in the first of Bejou and Bejou's (2016) nine suggestions. Students, staff, alumni, and other stakeholders must also be meaningfully included in shared governance if institutions are to achieve the fullest benefit from a process that requires considerable time and effort.

It is not uncommon for institutions and systems of higher education to have a statement or policy which outlines a working construct of shared governance and a commitment to that construct. If such a statement does not already exist, one ought to be developed collaboratively by all stakeholders. If one does exist, when was it last reviewed, revised (if desired), and reaffirmed? How often do such reviews of the statement take place, and who is responsible for initiating or facilitating it?

How can student affairs professionals help with regard to the development and ongoing vitality of goals for shared governance? First, be familiar with the local statement (if one exists) and the process through which it is periodically revisited (if one exists). Second, encourage all stakeholders and structures to be similarly aware. Working from a genuine perspective of inquiry and advocacy for a process, rather than from one of trying to put forward a particular model or method, can be an effective strategy.

MODELING PATIENCE AND COMMITMENT

Shared governance is not easy. It is not quick. It is not clean or pristine. It takes time, patience, and determination. "In one sense the governance of [the] university is governance by conversation. Many of the seemingly critical matters, such as the form of the curriculum or even the size of the budget . . . are the subject of thousands of hours of consultation and conversation before a final decision is ratified" (Mayhew, 1974, p. 58). While one may be readily willing to invest all those hours in a conversation one believes to be a matter of importance, it is important to be equally prepared to spend time on subjects for which one does not immediately see the value or need for great deliberation. Shared governance is not about me; it is about we.

That same principle of patience applies to being prepared for conversations which include all those whose voices ought to be heard. It is not enough to assume that other parties will know that they have an opportunity to contribute; reaching out to include stakeholders and allowing them the time to consider the question and develop their thoughts sends a signal that their participation is desired and valued. Cohen and March (1974) point out, "most people in a college are most of the time less concerned with the content of a decision than they are with eliciting an acknowledgement of their importance within the community" (p. 121).

Respecting diverse, and at times divergent, voices requires an openness to perspectives and positions which may not initially comport to given notions of professional or scholarly communication. Genuineness and thoughtfulness ought to be the measures of quality for contributions to shared discussions.

The principle of patience becomes particularly important at times of greater stress at the institution or in the system. The perception of higher stakes and greater urgency can lead to retrenchment or retreat from shared governance (Bahls, 2014). Doing so, however, undermines trust and conveys a message that shared governance is only a matter of convenience for the more mundane matters.

The willingness to engage in shared governance continuously and consistently is evidence of genuine commitment to it. Horvath (2017) observes, "Valuing shared governance means genuinely believing that what is created or determined collaboratively is better than what any individual might achieve" (p. 25).

Student affairs professionals can readily model both patience and commitment in matters of shared governance. Here are three simple tips for use in strengthening consideration of topics: agree on reasonable time frame for investigation, discussion, and development of input or decision; establish clear rules of engagement (how exactly will the process proceed); and close the loop (review/follow up after input or decision) (Goodman, 2017).

With regard to process, another way to help is to support meeting rules which allow for the collective development of agendas and which assure that meetings are held when all members can be present. We have probably all witnessed meetings schedule for when student members are on break or when staff or faculty are overwhelmed with their responsibilities at the beginning or end of a term.

Promoting Procedural Justice

The exercise of patience and commitment may help lead to positive perceptions of procedural justice related to shared governance at an institution or within a system of institutions (recall the discussion of social exchange and justice theories from Chapter One). Birnbaum clearly and thoroughly describes the importance of procedural justice as follows:

> Procedural justice refers to the perceived fairness of processes through which organizational decisions are made. Fair processes may be desirable in all organizations, but they are of particular importance in normative organizations, such as colleges and universities, in which goals are unclear and the consequences of decisions are not easily assessed. Unable to obtain reliable feedback on decision outcomes, participants in what Deal and Kennedy (1982) term these "process cultures" instead focus their attention on how things are done." (Birnbaum, 2004, p. 12)

Linking procedural justice, status, social capital, and social regulation, Birnbaum goes on to describe ways in which perceptions of procedural justice can be fostered or hindered:

> Decisions made in social systems are more likely to be accepted when the procedures creating them are seen as legitimate and fair. What is considered fair is related to the expectations of people involved in the process, expectations that are learned through the process of socialization.
>
> People are more likely to defer to the moral authority of structures and processes when they are developed so as to be consistent with existing social norms. Procedures or sanctions seen as illegitimate may lead not only to noncompliance, but to disrespect for the system that created them. Additional procedures, also see as illegitimate, may be created to respond to noncompliance, thus reducing even further the influence of authorities.
>
> Changes in social systems are more likely to be accepted when they do not challenge the social status of participants in that system and are less likely to be accepted when they do.
>
> Systems that provide forums in which people can interact on matters related to their group norms and personal values help to create dense networks of interaction that increase social capital within the system. Higher levels of social capital, in turn, lead to increased trust and cooperation, which are related to organizational differences.
>
> Informal social controls may be more effective than formal legal controls in influencing social compliance with organizational values. The strength of those informal controls will decline as the frequency of interaction within organizations decreases.
>
> Attempts to design utilitarian systems to increase organizational effectiveness may instead reduce effectiveness because they are inconsistent with participants' sense of what is proper. (Birnbaum, 2004, pp. 15–16)

How then can student affairs professionals help promote a sense of procedural justice related to shared governance? One significant way is to help make available forums and opportunities to develop the rich social connections which Birnbaum describes as central to the shaping and sustenance of social norms. This sort of thing should be a welcome challenge for student affairs professionals who typically spend a good deal of thought, time, and effort related to developing a sense of campus community. Boyer's (1990) six characteristics of community are an excellent framework for supporting a climate that lends itself to improving the likelihood of positive perceptions of procedural justice in matters of shared governance. As a reminder, the six characteristics are: purposeful, open, just, disciplined, caring, and celebrative. A more rich campus social fabric with plentiful opportunities to articulate and celebrate the norms for collaborative problem solving, difficult conversations, and ideas of campus citizenship can provide build social capital within the institution and help assure a strong foundation upon which shared governance can be practiced.

Developing and Sustaining Trust

No matter how purposeful and thoughtful the effort there are likely to come times when members of the campus community involved directly or indirectly in campus shared governance conversations find themselves with mixed feelings about exactly how those conversations are playing themselves out. In those moments of doubt, when perceptions can slide one way or the other, trust can be a critical difference in which way those perceptions move.

Pope (2004) defines trust as "an element in a consensual relationship in which there is equal risk and equal benefit as perceived by the parties involved, and there is a belief that the other party will act in a reciprocal manner" (p. 76) and, citing the work of Rosseau, Sitkin, Burt, and Camerer, Pope (2004) adds trust is a "willingness to be vulnerable to the actions of another party based on the expectations that that party will perform action of importance" (p. 76). Research has identified a number of benefits to trust in organizations, particularly at times of crisis (Pope, 2004).

Birnbaum (2004) emphasizes the important of establishing and maintaining trust in shared governance, describing it as an "essential component of democratic governance" (p.15). Drawing on the work of Braithwaite, Birnbaum describes several forms of trust. One of these is exchange trust which is "based on that authority's ability to compete successfully for and allocate resources" (Birnbaum, 2005, p. 15). Birnbaum observes that exchange trust is forward-looking in nature. Communal trust, which is based on "the ability to predict the authority's behavior because of a social connectedness that leads to shared norms and shared social identity" (Birnbaum, 2004, p. 15) is backward-looking. One can readily see how both exchange trust and communal trust can be related to considerations of procedural justice.

Zucker's (1986) work in describing three forms of trust is also illuminating with regard to shared governance. The first of the three forms is characteristic-based trust which comes about through social similarity and cultural congruence. The second, process-based trust, comes about through repeated interactions between parties. Institution-based trust, the third and final of Zucker's forms, is the product of impersonal formal social structures.

When added to the insights of Birnbaum (2004) and Zucker (1986) on forms of trust, Mihra's (as cited in Pope, 2004) identification of four components of trust is particularly helpful. Those components include: competence, openness, benevolence, and reliability. Pope (2004) notes others have suggested honesty as fifth component.

Unfortunately, the various parties involved in shared governance are too often lacking in trust for one another. Why? Bahls (2014) points to gaps in knowledge by boards about faculty and vice versa. "It is not surprising that these gaps in knowledge are often filled by unsubstantiated assumptions about the "others" that are significant obstacles to the kinds of mutual respect and trust essential to effective shared governance" (Bahls, 2014, p. 7). It is not unreasonable to assume that the same ignorance extends to the dynamics between other groups of stakeholders as well.

Like fostering community, building trust is nothing new to student affairs professionals. Adherence to Kitchener's (1984) five ethical principles (autonomy, justice, beneficence, nonmaleficence, and fidelity) are a bedrock of practice in the field, and those practices are all powerful strategies to developing the forms and components of trust as described by Birnbaum (2004), Zucker (1986), and Pope (2004). For sake of clarity, let us reframe those five principles in language specifically related to what we have learned to this point about shared governance. First, we ought to respect and value the independent role of all stakeholders in shared governance and respect their decisions without undue efforts to insert ourselves inappropriately in their deliberations. Second, we ought to assure that processes are fair equitable, and inclusive. Third, our efforts ought to be focused on helping others be engaged in decision-making which benefits themselves and the institution rather than on serving any of our self-interests. Fourth, as we engaged in shared governance and the conflicts which sometimes are an element of those processes, our thoughts should be on reaching a better conclusion rather than to defeating an opponent. Fifth and finally, as student affairs professionals our loyalties throughout shared governance conversations must remain with serving our institution through serving and supporting our students.

GETTING COMFORTABLE WITH POWER, POLITICS, AND PERSUASION

The tensions and conflict inherent in shared governance have been mentioned several times already in opening chapters of this book. It has to be recognized shared governance is, among other things, a political process. Cramer (2017) wryly comments, "Governance is like anchovies–it is something people either love or hate" (p. xv), and that bimodal distribution may in no small part be a reflection of the political nature of the beast. It is unfortunate but understandable that politics has such a negative connotation in our society and in the student affairs profession. Too many of our role models in what might be labeled the formal political arena leave a lot to be desired, and too many student affairs professionals either are not comfortable with or do not recognize the power they have and their abilities in political action. While it is difficult to be overly hopeful about the formal political arena, it is the goal of this section of Chapter Three to encourage change with regard to the relationship of readers to political behavior and the dynamics of political behavior in shared governance.

Defining and Describing Key Terms

This section will define and describe three key terms for the chapter. Those terms are politics, power, and persuasion.

Politics. For many, Sir Ernest John Pickstone's definition of politics resonates. "Politics is the art of looking for trouble, finding it whether it exists or not, diagnosing it incorrectly, and applying the wrong remedies" (Spring, 1944, p. 31). The term *politics* may, however, be defined in several more sanguine ways. It can refer to any of the following:

1a. the art or science of government
b: the art or science concerned with guiding or influencing governmental policy

c: the art or science concerned with winning and holding control over a government
2: political actions, practices, or policies
3a: political affairs or business especially: competition between competing interest groups or individuals for power and leadership (as in a government)
b: political life especially as a principal activity or profession
c: political activities characterized by artful and often dishonest practices
4: the political opinions or sympathies of a person
5a: the total complex of relations between people living in society
b: relations or conduct in a particular area of experience especially as seen or dealt with from a political point of view office politics ethnic politics. (Politics, n.d.)

Shared governance as practiced on most campuses is political as described in all five of the senses of the word as just discussed. Specifically, with regard to higher education and shared governance, Miller and Nadler (2006a) state, "The confluence of forces who believe that they are entitled to make decisions results is a highly interactive, fluid process of governance and decision making. Primary and secondary groups form coalitions that develop to impact decision making, and at other times, these groups are individual and isolated, in direct competition for resource or policy formation" (p. 14). "Whatever else organizations may be (problem-solving instruments, sociotechnical systems, reward systems, and so on), they are political structures. This means that organizations operate by distributing authority and setting a stage for the exercise of power" (Zaleznik, 1970, ¶2).

Power. Which brings us to offering a definition of *power.* Many people's first thought is about control or coercion. Weber's (1947) classic definition of power certainly comports to that view. He explains power as the likelihood that one will be able to exercise their will no matter the resistance. Weber (1958) describes three forms or types of power (economic, social, and political) and lists three forms of authority for power (traditional, charismatic, and legal rationale). The traditional form of authority stems from tradition or custom. The charismatic form comes from the personal characteristics of a given individual. Legal-rationale authority accords with notions of bureaucracy and hierarchy; it flows from legal and structural positions.

Morgan (2006) provides another helpful typology of power. Those types and brief notes on each follow:

1. Formal authority–akin to Weber's (1958) notion of legal-rationale authority, flows from position supported by legal authority
2. Control of scarce resources–ability to offer or withhold incentives or commodities
3. Uses of organizational structure, rules, and regulations–in colloquial terms, it is knowing how to play the system
4. Control of decision processes–for example, the ability to put something up for a vote, forward for signature, or out for payment
5. Control of knowledge and information–often overlooked as a type of power but increasingly important in many organizations, including higher education institutions and systems; having the keys to the data warehouse or insights into the thinking of key stakeholders are examples of this form of power
6. Control of boundaries–the ability to define the scope of responsibility for a unit or structure; the ability to set the agenda; or the ability to define who is considered a stakeholder and who is not are all examples of this form of power
7. Ability to cope with uncertainty–can be a personal or organizational trait; either way, it is the ability to be calm and be patient the full scope of the challenge or opportunity is not yet clearly known
8. Control of technology–can be a matter of being a gatekeeper or a matter of competence; either way, like information and knowledge, this is a very important but often unrecognized form of power in higher education
9. Interpersonal alliances and networks–alliances, coalitions, networks, and partnerships are essential in political environments
10. Control of counter-organizations–being the opposition is another often unrecognized source of power
11. Symbolism–the ability to define and draw on commonly recognized and understood cultural symbols which reflect deeply and strongly held communal values; much of how decisions and processes are perceived relates to their symbolic rather than their objective elements

Morgan's (2006) typology is very similar to another well-known set of the bases of power. French and Raven (1959) list the following as bases of power for leadership: legitimate (legal/positional), reward (control of resources), expert (knowledge or skills), referent (networks and alliances), and coercive (reward and punishment). Raven (1965) added information as a seventh item to the list.

There are important critical considerations to keep in mind when it comes to power. Various forms of power are often associated with privilege, both earned and unearned. A robust discussion of this idea is beyond the scope of this work, but readers are strongly encouraged to consider the ways in which race, class, gender, social class, and other dimension of human experience and identity play themselves out with regard to power, politics, and shared governance.

Power in and of itself is neither good nor bad. The way in which power is exercised may be good, bad, or some blend of those, and the perception of where that judgement falls is likely to vary across individuals and groups of individuals. The ethical exercise of power, which will call readers who are student affairs professionals back to the earlier discussion of Kitchener's principles (1984), is tremendously important in addressing both social justice and moral dimensions of the politics of shared governance. It is possible in this way to take advantage of what Giddens (1990) describes as the transformative capacity of power and to make a meaningful difference.

Persuasion. Simply put, persuasion may be understood as the process through which one exercises power in the interest of personal or political goals. Here, for our purposes in this chapter, we focus on the political act of persuasion.

Aristotle (2004), the Greek philosopher, described three elements of persuasion: logic (*logos*), ethics (*ethos*), and emotion (*pathos*). Logic refers to both the strength and quality of your argument. Ethos reflects your believability, character, and integrity. Pathos is soul or spirit of your position.

Silverman (2000) identifies five elements of persuasion in more contemporary business terms, but those contemporary terms have strong semblance to Aristotle's ideas. Source, the first of Silverman's elements, is comparable to ethos. The second element is message, and Silverman's (2000) description of it calls to mind both logos and pathos. It reflects both the merit of your position and the skill with which you convey it. The third element is medium, and it has no obvious Aristotelian counterpart. What will the vehicle be for your effort to bring someone to support your view–social media, print, formal speech, informal conversation, broadcast piece, video, or some other form? Knowing your audience, which Silverman (2000) identifies as the fourth element, is an acknowledgement that different aspects of an issue may resonate with various groups party to the discussion. The fifth and final element is effect, and it is arguably better understood as an outcome of persuasion rather than as an element of it.

Political Mapping

One recommendation for student affairs professionals to help them in becoming comfortable with politics, power, and persuasion is to get in the habit of political mapping. Such maps may take on varying levels of detail and sophistication, but a fairly simple and straightforward version will suffice in most instances to assist student affairs professionals in collecting and organizing thoughts related to the political process for a given shared governance issue. Figure 3.1 below is an example of a simple political map.

The question at hand as mapped in Figure 3.1 is a proposed increase in the technology fee charged to students. Arrayed around the question are boxes noting the various stakeholders in the discussion; their likelihood to engage on the question at what level and from what perspective(s); the sources of power held by those strength holders; and notes on how they might be persuaded to come to a position of supporting the increase in the fee. The chart also shows the anticipated discussion and political interaction between the various stakeholders. Unidirectional arrows indicate advice, input, and persuasion flowing in a given direction; bidirectional arrows indicate a sharing of advice, input, and persuasion back and forth between parties.

It is critically important when creating a political map that you identify the true question at hand. Many readers have likely been party to discussions or disputes which might appear to the casual observer to be about one thing, but the reality as recognized by those familiar with the context of the discourse is that the apparent topic is really a proxy for another underlying issue. Reconsidering for a moment the example pictured in Figure 3.1, the question of the proposed increase in technology fee might be a symptom of a larger concern about enrollment management strategy at the institution as it relates to pricing position in the competitive marketplace. Alterna-

Figure 3.1. Example of Political Map

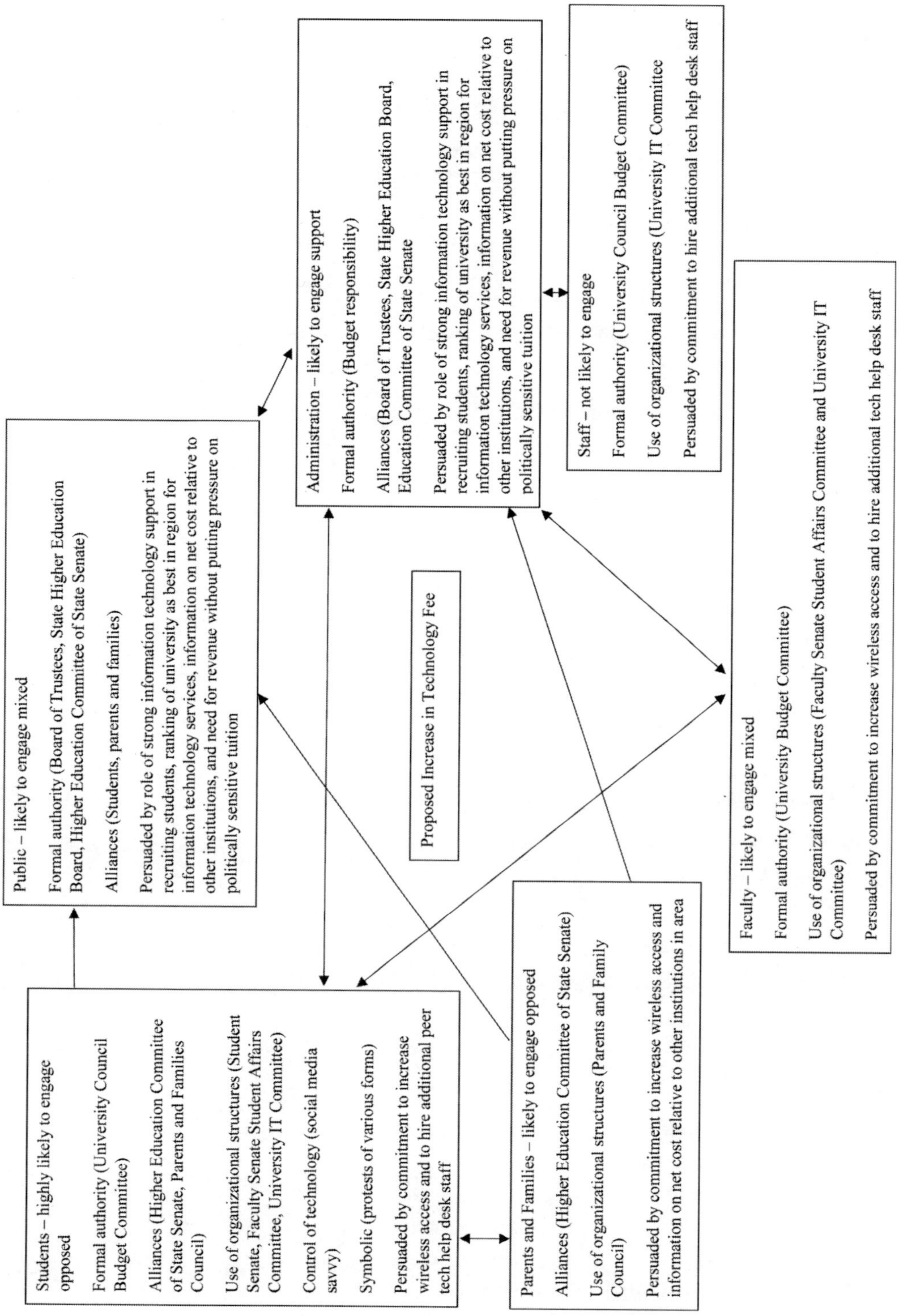

tively, it could be just the last straw in a question about the budgeting process at the institution and how shared governance should work there. Anyone who is interested in making use of political mapping as a tool for better understanding politics, power, and persuasion at their institution needs to consider the context and the reflect thoughtfully on the central question at hand before they begin charting out stakeholders, sources of power, and possible lines of persuasion.

Words of Wisdom

The words of two philosophers offer helpful advice with regard to the practice of politics, power, and persuasion. Too many are ignorant about what politics is, who the players are, and how they think and act. Our ignorance of these things and our antipathy for what we perceive politics to be leads us to fear behaving in ways that are seen as political. This leads us to the advice of our first philosopher Yoda, the Jedi Master. He reminds us, "Fear is the path to the Dark Side. Fear leads to anger, anger leads to hate, hate leads to suffering" (Kurtz & Lucas, 1977). Seek to understand the answers to the who, why, and how of shared governance, and assume the best of others while moving through this exploration. Just as Yoda encouraged young Luke to enter the cave to confront his fear, so too should we move forward into the realm of political thought and action.

How should we behave as we take those steps into what may seem like murky and troubled territory? The words of Bruce Lee, martial arts master, offer a thoughtful and useful approach. "Be like water making its way through cracks. Do not be assertive, but adjust to the object, and you shall find a way around or through it. If nothing within you stays rigid, outward things will disclose themselves" (Little & Lee, 2000).

ENCOURAGING FULL (BUT NOT TOO FULL) PARTICIPATION

Effective shared governance requires the participation of many individuals and groups of individuals. Having any one party underrepresented or overrepresented, either numerically or in level of engagement, results in a diminishment of the result in product, process, or both a sort of tragedy of the commons (Lloyd, 1833) and an inverse form of that same dilemma.

Striking the right balance is particularly important in organizations where there is a wide array of power and status levels (Lizzio & Wilson, 2009). The challenge is both a matter of getting people into the process and, once there, having all those in the process to be fully involved in ways that respect their roles and their personhood.

It seems that in any group or organization of people there are always a few people who are interested in being involved in almost every aspect of governance, and their reasons for doing so vary. Some may be supercitizens who see themselves as having a responsibility to take part, believe they are the only ones (or one of a select few) who have what it takes to get the job done, or are seeking the opportunity to develop knowledge, networks, or skills that will help them in the future. There are others in any group or organization who are willing to be involved on a more selective basis with their participation varying based on activity or topic at hand, their current circumstances within the group or organization (for example, how heavy is their workload at the moment or do they see their involvement as supported within their unit), and personal factors. Finally, and unfortunately, the largest group of people in a group or organization is made up of those who are not inclined at any time to become involved. Their inclination may reflect a sense of alienation or powerlessness, lack of awareness about how to be involved or lack of self-confidence in being able to contribute anything of value, perceived vulnerability or disincentive within their unit with regard to participation, or personal circumstances (for example, they may be pursuing a degree in their hours away from work so they have no energy for another project).

Goodman (2017) notes, "In order to encourage faculty, staff, and students to get involved in shared governance, it is necessary to demonstrate that many of their personal and professional goals and aims have a direct connection to the current and long-term goals of the governance organization" (p. 246). It may, however, be a bit more complicated than merely helping people see link between their goals and their engagement. Here the work of Vroom (1964) on expectancy theory can be a helpful model for considering how student affairs professionals (and others) can help people in identifying motivation to participate in shared governance processes. Vroom argues that motivation is a function of the interaction of three variables—*valence, expectancy,* and *instrumentality*. Valence can be thought of as the value an individual places on a particular outcome or goal. Valence increases when an outcome is more clear (or specific) and more salient (more important to the individual). For example, a community college staff member may want to see the institution take greater care of its entry-level clerical and service employees. That is a goal with a good deal of salience for them, but it could benefit from some greater clarity. What does "take good care" mean for them? A discussion about what that might look like could lead to a number of specific goals, including developing a policy allowing for the gifting of unused vacation or sick days. Expectancy might be described as understanding that a particular pathway will lead to the desired goal or outcome. Our community college staff member now has significant valence when it comes to seeing a leave gifting policy being implemented but may not see a way in which they can bring this about. Helping them identify the shared governance processes where that work can take place can foster greater expectancy. Instrumentality is a person's sense of the likelihood that they can successfully pursue a given pathway to the goal or outcome. That sense of instrumentality can be understood as having three components. First, does the person see themselves as having the knowledge and skills necessary to be successful? Second, does the person have a sense of a locus of internal control or self-efficacy with regard to the pathway? Third, does the person believe that the system is set up in such a way that a person like themselves (however they construct their identities) has a chance to succeed in that pathway?

Conversations about valence and expectancy are helpful and relatively straightforward. Conversations about instrumentality, and in particular about the third component of instrumentality, are much more complex. A word of caution is in order for colleagues considering encouraging others to be involved in shared governance. Oppression and privilege are real, and they play themselves out in higher education organizations as they do throughout American society. It is vitally important to respect all forms of diversity and to ensure that representation at the table is inclusive and meaningful (Horvath, 2017).

In addition, while students are typically protected in their shared governance activities by the code of student conduct and relevant law and faculty are protected by the tradition of academic freedom and (at least some faculty) by collective bargaining or tenure, staff are particularly vulnerable when it comes to having some sense of surety that speaking up and speaking out in the course of shared governance will not be held against them in future employment considerations. The climate and values of the institution must affirm and protect the right all stakeholders to speak freely and without fear of recrimination, and student affairs professionals can be advocates, guardians, and models for ethical and inclusive behavior.

AVOIDING COMMON MISTAKES

Our attention to this point has been focused on things we might do that could foster and strengthen shared governance, but there are some things that student affairs professionals and other administrative staff might do that would inhibit shared governance. Tierney (2003) lists seven such practices:

1. Convene a group, invest them with authority, then do not implement their decisions
2. Ask for input and ignore it
3. Be reactive rather than proactive
4. Set rules for mutual governing but feel free to ignore or break them
5. Seek input from exclusive sources
6. Fail to provide professional development or support to faculty in leadership roles
7. Limit resources and discourage external comparison opportunities

Here again, it should be noted that providing professional development and support for staff and faculty in leadership roles is important in much the same way as Tierney notes that it is for faculty.

ADHERING TO GOOD ADVICE

Bahls (2014) discussed desired characteristics of shared governance with presidents, trustees, and faculty members. Seven key words appeared time and again in the remarks that were shared. Those words are: trust; collaboration; communication; transparency; inclusiveness; honesty; and integrity. It seems the concepts reflected in those words would be appreciated by all stakeholders in shared governance and are ones which student affairs professionals at all career levels can model in their behavior.

Returning our focus to the ways in which we can have a positive effect and in keeping with the words from Bahls' (2014) conversations, Horvath (2017) describes nine practical tips for working with shared governance structures and processes. Several of them have been touched on already, but they bear repeating. The nine tips are:

1. Set a realistic timeline
2. Work with campus leadership to identify stakeholders
3. Use existing governance structures effectively
4. Engage people who are new arrivals and those with depth of experience
5. Be transparent about the process
6. Provide multiple chances for input
7. Respond to suggestions
8. Collect and use data
9. Communicate a consistent message

Adding to the nine practical tips, Horvath (2017) mentions two tactical suggestions which serve as a strong conclusion for this chapter. First, "embrace the messy, tangled parts of democratic action all the words and positions and conjecturing and arguing" (p. 25). Second, and very importantly in terms of taking on a role in helping to strengthening shared governance, "believe that it can be learned" (p. 25).

REFLECTION QUESTIONS

1. Using Bejou and Bejou's (2016) nine suggestions, how strong do you believe your institution's shared governance practices to be?
2. What are the areas of strength and weakness when it comes to trust on your campus?
3. How might you help assure continued trust where it already exists and enhanced trust where there is room for improvement?

4. What have your experiences and perceptions been with regard to political activity on your campus?
5. How proficient at politics do you believe yourself to be?
6. What are your sources of power in your campus role?
7. How do you see the level of participation across stakeholder groups in shared governance on your campus?
8. Are there particular groups of people who you feel are not fully participating in shared governance on your campus? If so, what do you believe are the barriers to their participation?
9. Identify a specific shared governance question or issue on your campus and develop a political map for it.
10. Develop an action plan for you to pursue in helping foster and strengthen shared governance on your campus.

Chapter 4

STUDENT PARTICIPATION IN SHARED GOVERNANCE

While conscious efforts are routinely made to protect students' rights in university policy and procedures, the often hierarchical structures of educational institutions can, perhaps inadvertently, privilege 'staff discourse' and marginalise student views.

Levin and Wilson (2009, p. 71)

Grand Old University, Can You Hear Us?

Grand Old University (GOU) has a rich, storied, and in some ways problematic history. What began as a state normal school has grown to become the flagship institution for the southern state's higher education system. It has seen its reputation for research, technology and knowledge transfer, and academic quality steadily rise over the past few decades even as it has struggled to also address the sociohistoric challenges of racism and economic disparities which continue to play themselves out in challenging ways at the institution as well as in the state. The student body of GOU reflects those challenges in a number of ways, and the school has a reputation (fair or not) for being a haven for the more financially fortunate sons and daughters of the state's and region's White families. GOU's undergraduate student governing body is substantially driven by members of the campus' active and highly visible Greek community, and most of the body's appointments to the various campus governance structures are students who are members of sororities and fraternities at GOU. Little attention has been paid through the years to GOU's graduate and professional students when it comes to shared governance at the university.

Recently the GOU undergraduate senate has become concerned because it is finding it increasingly difficult to identify students who are willing to fill the various spots on university committees, and there has been a growing need for mid-year replacement as students who have agreed to take on certain roles have stepped away from them. Those students have cited personal reasons or a sense of their time (which they see as very limited) as being wasted.

At the same time as this issue is coming to the surface within the GOU undergraduate government, the leader of the institution's faculty senate has sought out the vice president for student affairs to share frustration that student members of the various university committees are not being appointed in a timely fashion, are not being active in their service, or are abandoning their appoints. The faculty leader sees this as presenting an added burden on faculty who feel that they need to speak on behalf of students when students themselves are not present. He wonders aloud if students might not be more interested in padding their résumés than in playing an active role in shared governance.

The vice president asks the chairs of campus committees to let her office know of any open student spots on their committees which need to be filled and to share the names of student members who either seem disengaged or who have walked away entirely. Recognizing a number of the names on the list as students who are active in a number of campus organizations and programs and with whom she feels she has established a relationship, the vice chancellor decides to reach out to them to learn more about what is going on with regard to their service on committees. She gets feedback very similar to that which the leadership of GOU's undergraduate senate is receiving. Much of what is discussed is not important to students, and the committees do not seem to be all that concerned with meaningfully incorporating student feedback. Student members are treated politely, but there is not much learning or opportunity to have a real impact so students are tuning out and turning elsewhere.

The vice president mentions these developments in an executive staff meeting as an issue that is going to need to be addressed. There is little reaction from her colleagues to this item of business, but the university ombudsperson shares that she has been approached at least a half dozen times over the past year by students representing various campus groups seeking advice on how they can have their voices heard in shared governance. These students report that they feel shutout of the opportunities because they are not senators and, as non-Greeks and persons from historically marginalized groups, they feel they are unlikely to be able to become senators.

The vice chancellor leaves the executive staff meeting with more questions than answers. Those questions all center around how can she and her colleagues in student affairs help students be fully involved in shared governance at GOU.

It should be apparent to readers by now that student affairs professionals can play an important role in fostering and strengthening shared governance at their institutions. That role can be particularly critical when it comes to helping assure the full participation of students in a host of structures and processes. As Levin (2009) observes, "in the highest levels of institutional decision making, students and student interests are not necessarily the central concerns" (Levin, 2009, p. 45). However, those interests and concerns are cornerstones of student affairs practice along with student development and learning.

This chapter will offer a brief history of student participation in shared governance as well as information on the degree to which students are (or are not involved) in shared governance in contemporary practice. Strategies for making the case for greater student involvement will be offered as will information on the potential benefits to students from participating in shared governance and strategies for working directly with students to encourage and support them in taking part. The chapter concludes by presenting several important open questions about students and shared governance in American higher education.

History of Student Participation

There is a long and interesting history of student involvement in helping manage the affairs of higher education organizations, though uneven and uncertain at points along the way. This section of the chapter briefly describes that history.

Student participation in higher education governance predates the American colonies. According to Miller and Nadler (2006b), "college students have been involved in different aspects of running higher education institutions since the rise of student nations at Bologna" (p. 9). However, "the role of students in higher education has waxed and waned since the establishment of the academy" (Ryan, 2017, p. 71).

That participation began in the earliest days of American higher education with students at the first campuses in our nation.

> Beginning with institutions in the eastern United States, students formed their governance bodies or roles outside the formal structure of the institution, and often in response to poor conditions with the college. Fraternities developed because of institutional mismanagement of residence halls, guilds and literary societies were formed in response to bad teaching, clubs were formed around book collections because of the poor library collections, and athletic teams were developed because of the college's concentration solely on cognitive development. (Miller & Nadler, 2006b, pp. 9–10)

While some steps were taken before the Civil War to establish centralized governing structures, those efforts expanded and took deeper root in the late nineteenth century (Crowly, 1980). Student involvement in governance grew as shared governance became increasingly common at institutions and with other changes (including the formation of an elective system for courses) taking place in American higher education (Miller & Nadler, 2006b).

The development of student senates was a natural outcome of the growth of shared governance and student involvement in institutional governance. As Miller and Nadler (2006b) describe, "student governments were brought to life at U.S. institutions by university officials in the early 20th century in order to help address student behavior issues with the intention of opening up lines of communication and engaging student leaders as proxies or allies in the effort" (p. 2).

The formation of national student government organizations was one outcome of the rise in the number of student senates. The United States National Students Association was formed in 1947 at the University of Washington. It merged with the National Student Lobby in 1978 and formed the United States Student Association (USSA, 1980).

The next substantive change in the nature of student involvement in campus governance took place in the 1960s and 1970s. Coupled with a decline in the in loco parentis relationship between institutions and students and an increase in student expectations with regard to a voice in institutional governance, student organizations and student senates were taking up important social issues and having a significant impact on policy and practice at both the campus and national levels. One shared governance outcome of this period of student activism was the inclusion of student positions on central shared governance structures at the institutional and state level. Writing at the time, Alexander (1969) observed, "the recent threats of student power activists have set in motion a host of plans to place more students within the decision-making structures of colleges and universities across the nation" (p. 39). Another shared governance structural outcome was the development of graduate student unions (Bray, 2006).

Following this period of widespread focus on social activism, the attention of student senates turned inward on matters at hand on individual campuses. "In the 60s and 70s the emphasis many student government deliberations and actions was on the social movements and political matters at hand, but in subsequent years "the focus shifted from political issues to campus based issues, including the raising of tuition and student fees, library hours, and parking" (Miller & Nadler, 2006b, p. 2).

Contemporary Context of Students in Shared Governance

Having reviewed the history of student involvement in shared governance, we now turn our attention to contemporary conditions and practices. Students impact higher education decision-making through three mechanisms: self-governing structures; reactions to policies and practices; and stands on public issues taken by student groups (Cowley, 1980). Our attention in this section will be on those self-governing structures, but it is worth noting that students may also engage in these other ways perhaps with even greater effect at times. Examples of student action at the campus level include the student protests around some campus monuments or building names (the Silent Sam statue at the University of North Carolina or the call to rename the Ed Meek School of Journalism and New Media at the University of Mississippi as examples of such protests) and student responses to invited speakers who they find objectionable. One national study of incoming college freshman found that nearly 10 percent expect to participate in protests while in college (New, 2016), and one need only to look to student action and leadership in movements such as voter registration and public facilities integration in the 1960s or to Black Lives Matter and Me Too in the early twenty-first century.

As noted in Chapter Two, student self-governance structures can be categorized as either central (those addressing broad student affairs issues) or as peripheral (those dealing with specific sub-units or issues) (Cowley, 1980). "Students often have their own network of parallel undergraduate and graduate governance organizations headed by a student body president and elected representatives that have contact with university officials, such as the president and the board" (Pusser & Loss, 2018, ¶22). The central structures, while common, are not always viewed in a positive light. "Student governance, despite its 60-year history, has struggled in recent years to overcome a stigma of ineffectiveness. These bodies have been further plagued with lower voter turnout during elections and an across-the-board perspective that participation is meaningless" (Miller, 2006, p. 70).

Unfortunately, the assessment of student involvement in institutional or state shared governance structures is similarly disappointing. "Historically students have not had a significant role in the organizational structure or governance of colleges and universities" (Pusser & Loss, 2018, ¶21). Ryan (2017) comments, "While students have forced their way into conversations on various topics (within a wide range, including athletics, changes in curriculum, and sexual assault policies), there has yet to be a significant shift toward student involvement in formal governing boards" (p. 73). In a study done very late in the twentieth century, Jones and Skolnik (1997) found that faculty and students made up more than 25 percent of membership of boards for Canadian institutions but less than 3 percent for U.S. institutions. Davis (2006) cites research indicating 30 of 53 statewide regulatory coordinating boards had student members (25 were voting) and just over half of the boards the boards of trustees had a student member. Still "little evidence can be found that higher education governance has progressed beyond "tokenism" and embraced the potential role and contributions that be made by student trustees" (Davis, 2006, p. 90).

This is not to say that there are no examples of meaningful student participation in institutional self-governance. Marlboro College in Vermont is having success in making shared governance, including robust student participation, an important principle of its community. "A lot of colleges talk up shared governance, but nobody does it like Marlboro, where everyone on campus–from the janitor to the president–can propose changes and vote on them at weekly town meetings. At Marlboro, students are full citizens of the campus community, sitting on committees that evaluate instructors, draft admissions policies, and develop curricula. They even chair the Selectboard, which sets the agenda for town meetings" (Field, 2018, ¶3).

Making the Case

So how do those of us who believe in the importance of student involvement in shared governance advocate to help bring it about at our institutions or in American higher education more broadly? The literature of the field offers a number of useful thoughts on this question.

The AAUP (1967) *Statement on Government of Colleges and Universities* specifically addresses the importance of engaging students in shared governance, though noting that students do not currently play a significant role.

> Students are referred to in this statement as an institutional component coordinate in importance with trustees, administrators, and faculty. There is, however, no main section on students. The omission has two causes: (1) the changes now occurring in the status of American students have plainly outdistanced the analysis by the educational community, and an attempt to define the situation without thorough study might prove unfair to student interests, and (2) students do not in fact at present have significant voice in the government of colleges and universities; it would be unseemly to obscure, by superficial equality of length of statement, what may be a serious lag entitled to separate and full confrontation. (AAUP, 1967, ¶3)

Clark and Trow (1966) caution that a disengaged student government "closes a main avenue of involvement–a road that encourages identification with the college and involvement with ideas" (pp. 51–52). In contrast, an active student government has been described as helpful to the quality of student life (Carnegie Foundation for the Advancement of Teaching, 1990).

Austin and Jones (2016) posit four arguments for the inclusion of students in shared governance. The first of these is *political realism.* Students are stakeholders and politically-significant constituents in higher education, and "policy formation and decision making in higher education is a largely political process that is reliant on representative groups to represent larger issues. Such a context relates a compelling argument in favor of an organized student voice and representation" (Miller & Nadler, 2006b, p. 14). The second is of *consumerism* (Austin & Jones, 2016). Students ought to be in position to safeguard their interests as the consumers of services. Murdock (2006) "The primary consumers of institutions of higher education are the students. While students may not always be paying for their expenses at colleges and universities, they are the reason that these educational institutions exist, and because of this, students ought to have a voice in how an institution functions" (Murdock, 2006, p. 117). *Communitarianism* is the third of Austin and Jones' (2016) four. Higher education at its best is a cooperative enterprise of all involved. The fourth argument focuses on *democracy and consequentialism.* Engaging students in shared governance fosters both, and that is one of the important purposes of American higher education.

Lizio and Wilson (2009) identify three practical perspectives which inform efforts to argue for meaningful student participation in shared governance: "functional (how does it benefit the university?); developmental (how does it benefit the student?); and social (how does it benefit society?)" (p. 70).

Miller and Nadler (2006b) relate three broad roles for students in shared governance. Those roles are advocacy, representation, and giving voice. Miller and Nadler (2006b) also identify six arguments supporting student involvement in shared governance:

1. Students are entitled to citizenship on campus, and an essential part of citizenship is the franchise

2. Students are around about as long as the average term of a college president
3. Higher education is about learning; and students know it when they see it
4. Students learn from involvement
5. Students are more concerned about teaching and campus life than any other group
6. Preparing students for democracy

A Conceptual Model

While important, it is not enough for student affairs professionals to simply make the argument as to why students ought to be full partners in shared governance. We must also be prepared to help share thoughts on how that might look at our institutions. Zou and Ratosy (1999) present a conceptual model of student involvement in university decision making (Figure 4.1 below).

The model describes informal and formal interactions with a variety of stakeholders. It recognizes that students are both acting on and acted upon in the course of their participation in shared governance. Finally, it acknowledges that any plan to support the engaged of students in university decision making must be shaped by the unique circumstances of that institution in the contexts of the campus and general environments.

POTENTIAL BENEFITS TO STUDENTS

As noted in the preceding section, one of Lizio and Wilson's (2009) three perspectives on the involvement of students in shared governance is how does it benefit the student? Student affairs professionals are likely to be particularly drawn to this line of argument and are arguably uniquely positioned to make this case to students and others for the full participation of students in shared governance.

Kuh and Lund (1994) note, "assertions abound about the value of student involvement in institutional governance" (p. 5). They point out that student participation of this sort presents valuable opportunities to connect classroom learning to governance experiences as a way of strengthening learning. Kuh and Lund (1994) go on to identify a host

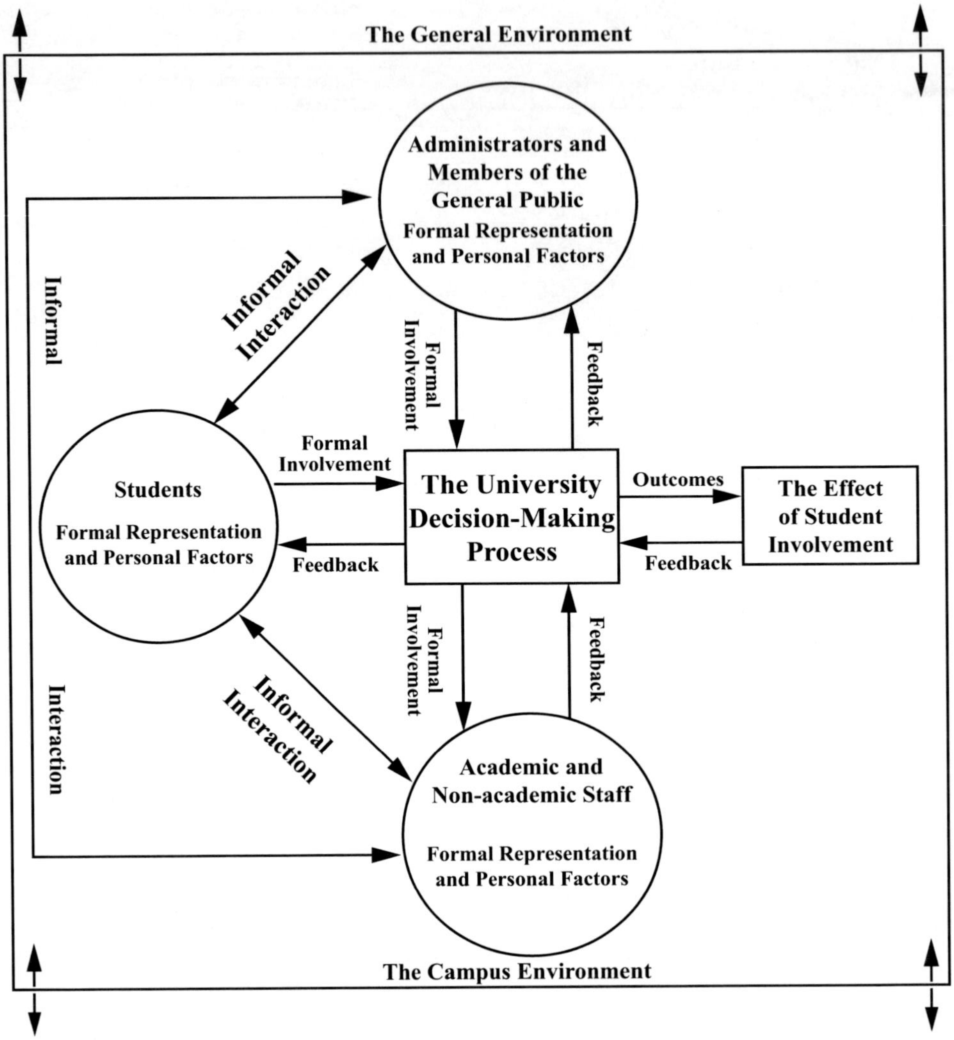

Figure 4.1. Conceptual Model of Student Involvement in University Decision Making

Source: From B. Zou and E. W. Ratosy (1999). Student participation in university governance. *Canadian Journal of Higher Education, 29*(1), 1–26. Reproduced by permission.

of direct and indirect effects which have been identified in various studies. Among these positive benefits to students are the following:

- Significant direct effect on women's choice of science occupations

- Significant indirect effects on both professional and nonprofessional occupations
- Significant positive direct effect on the humanitarian values of black men, white men, and white women
- Indirect effect on increasing the likelihood of a student's choice of a social service occupation
- Significant positive effect on students' perceived leadership competence and on academic, leadership and social-self-esteem of white women
- Significant positive direct effect on the social self-concept of black men and on students' academic, social, and artistic self-concept
- Positive indirect influence on the social self-concept of white women
- Positive direct effect on the persistence of white men, black men, and white women
- Short-term effects included increased stress levels, heightened awareness of ethical issues and dilemmas, and increased use of coping strategies
- Long-term effects include enhanced sense of moral awareness and personal responsibility

Barrett and Quarless (2017) powerfully articulate the potential ways in which students can develop and learn though their involvement.

> Shared governance has more than just a democratizing effect on students. Those who engage receive more attention and mentoring. They gain skills in leadership. They learn to communicate, organize, and advocate for their peers in settings where authority must be part of the solution. They learn to negotiate with power and to address both the positive and negative impacts of hierarchical and democratic decision making. . . . Students who engage in governance learn how to engage a community, enlist others, and work collectively to solve problems that cannot be solved by one person and to work for solutions that benefit an entire community. (p. 56)

Barrett and Quarless go on to point out that the benefits are even great for students from historically marginalized populations as involvement in shared governance can foster connections to faculty, staff, and other students.

Through enhancing academic and social integration (Tinto, 1993), promoting a sense of mattering (Rosenberg & McCullough, 1981), and encouraging developing social capital (Wells, 2008), student involvement in shared governance can also promote student persistence and retention. Mix (2013) offers an example of strengthening student success initiatives through participation in shared governance at South Dakota State University

ENCOURAGING AND SUPPORTING STUDENTS IN BEING INVOLVED

It is not enough as student affairs professionals to advocate that our institutions recognize students as full participants in shared governance and that we are aware of the potential benefits to students that may come about through such involvement. As Barrett and Quarless (2017) appropriately point out, "students have different obstacles to participation in governance. Recent years have seen an increase in the numbers of students both attending classes and working a substantial number of hours weekly" (p. 42). How do we as student affairs professionals actually support individual students in stepping into shared governance roles?

Miller and Nadler (2006b) describe a number of important institutional support for students serving in shared governance roles. Their suggestions are described and amplified upon below.

Trustworthy and Honest

The first of the institutional supports identified by Miller and Nadler (2006b) is a need for shared governance leaders to be trustworthy and honest in their dealings with one another. The importance of trust in shared governance was discussed at some length in Chapter Three, but it bears repeating here that it is tremendously important that students be able to trust those with whom they are dealing. This is particularly important given the extant power differential between the students and their faculty and administrative partners in the governance processes. It is no less important that other shared governance leaders come to see the students participating in the process as trustworthy and honest players.

Part and parcel of being trustworthy and honest is being genuine both about who you are and why you are involved. Students can smell hypocrisy faster than they smell pizza, and at the first whiff of the former they turn their trust elsewhere. If one is not completely committed to engaging students as full partners in shared governance, then it would be best not to engage in the mere window dressing for the sake of appearances. Students will recognize the disingenuous nature of the interaction, and they likely will either confront it or step away from it.

Advising

Bloland (1967) offers three domains or areas of advising student organizations and student leaders: maintenance, group growth, and program content (1967). It is important to take a moment here and acknowledge that the advisors helping students involved in student governance roles may or may not be student affairs professionals; they may also be faculty members or other administrative professionals on campus (Kane, 2017). Students moving into and through roles in shared governance can benefit greatly from competent and strong advising (Miller & Nadler, 2006b).

Competent advising requires that the person involved have an understanding of the shared governance shareholders, structures, and processes at the institution or in the systems. That person ought to also have a knowledge and skills related to the general principles and practices of advising. In the vernacular, the person playing the advising role should know their advising stuff.

Strong advising should not be confused with giving direction or instruction. The best advising is about how to think about an issue or question and not about what to think about it. In doing so, we are adhering to the ethical principle of respecting the autonomy of the student (Kitchener, 1984). The goal is to avoid any action or interaction as an advisor that may lead or shape the outcome of deliberation in a particular direction.

There may be times in the course of supporting students that they are angry or disappointed in decisions made or being contemplated at the university. There may also be times when the person supporting the student does not personally agree with the decision or the contemplated position. A strong and trustworthy advisor will also be honest about any conflict they have in offering advice and be transparent and proactive in helping assure the any actions or decisions are consistent with applicable institutional regulations. In this way the advisor can adhere to the ethical principle of loyalty (Kitchener, 1984).

Caring and Inclusive

The third type of institutional support identified by Miller and Nadler (2006b) is a caring and inclusive approach. There should be recognition and appreciation that any student deciding to become involved in shared governance is making a gift of time and energy to the institution, and that the time and energy are not always in abundant supply in the lives of students. At the same time they are giving this gift, they are taking on additional responsibility and attendant stress while opening themselves up to conflict and judgement at the same time they are trying to help their university and to learn valuable knowledge and skills. Knowing that at least one person at the institution sees this and cares about them as a person and as a student can be a powerfully positive support.

Inclusivity is another way of creating support for student involvement in shared governance. The gifts, risks, and rewards described in the preceding paragraph may all take on different degrees of salience or take somewhat different forms for students who are members of marginalized or minoritized populations. Reinforcing for these students that their identity and their involvement are not two distinct and disconnected things but rather interconnected and reciprocally shaping things may be invaluable.

Supporting students in being involved in shared governance does not mean speaking for students or on behalf of students. It means using your position at the institutions to open up spaces and to help assure that student voices can be heard.

Maintain Confidentiality

Students engaging in shared governance roles need to have people with whom they can share thoughts, ideas, reactions, and plans. This may be for the purposes of reality checking, testing out, or simply venting. The person who is approached may sometimes be the advisor to their organization, or it may be someone else at the institution. Whoever it may be, the student needs to know that what they share will be held in confidence wherever and whenever possible (Miller &

Nadler, 2006a). Without such support, the student may feel isolated and less able to effectively and fully participate in the process or decision at hand.

Build Relationships

The fifth and final of Miller and Nadler's (2006b) forms of institutional support is building relationships. Such relationships provide support for the student as a person and as a political player in shared governance. Of course, the development of relationships is not usually a function of happenstance. It is a matter of intention, commitment, and ongoing effort. As it relates to shared governance, it may well be a function of the environmental design of the campus (Strange & Banning, 2001) with people selected for certain roles based, at least in part, or their ability to build and sustain relationships and with spaces and campus cultures constructed in ways that foster the development of relationships.

Practical and Powerful Practices

In rounding out this section of the chapter, here are three practical and powerful practices to help support students be fully engaged in shared governance. Help secure institutional commitment to these three policies across the various governance structures at your institution, and you will be making an important contribution to supporting students in governance roles. First, student members will be involved in the setting of all agendas for the group and writing of all drafts for the group. This helps assure substantial and meaningful inclusion of students in processes rather than always having them be in a proactive rather than reactive position. Second, the majority of student members in the group must be present for any meeting to be held. This helps assure that students will be at the table when decisions are made. Third, students involved in substantial governance roles will be offered the opportunity for financial support in filling those roles (being careful not to compromise their integrity as representative voices for students). This will help assure that students from across a diversity of financial backgrounds will have a greater opportunity to be able to afford the time necessary to engaged in campus leadership.

OPEN QUESTIONS

There are a number of informal and formal ways for students to be involved in shared governance in American higher education (Lizio & Wilson, 2009). However, according to Miller and Nadler (2006b), "the role of student government in university and institutional governance remains an unanswered question among students and administrators" (p. 2), and "a primary question for institutions to address is what they expect from shared governance with students, and if they are not fulfilling that expectation, how they can be more meaningful and purposeful in defining a clear role and objectives for student governance" (p. 3). Answering this primary question will require that institutions have given meaningful thought to the role and nature of the student in the institution (Lizio & Wilson, 2009) as "the nature of student involvement and participation in institutional governance and decision-making are significantly determined by the institutions' conception of its and the definition of its student university relationship" (Austin & Jones, 2016, p. 142)

In addition to the open questions to be addressed at the institutional level, there is very little focus on students in the literature of shared governance (Zuo & Ratsoy, 1999). It would be very helpful to have current studies and scholarship of practice focused on what is the current state of affairs with regard to student involvement in shared governance? How do students experience that involvement? How do other shared governance partners view student involvement? What are the outcomes for them, the decisions made, and the institutions? Student affairs practitioners and others could do a great deal to help explore these important questions.

REFLECTION QUESTIONS

1. Following up on Miller and Nadler's (2006b) prompt, what does your institutions expect from shared governance with students? Is that expectation being met? If not, how can the institution be more meaningful and purposeful in defining a clear role and objectives for students and shared governance?
2. Lodge (2005) poses three questions as a framework for reflecting on shared governance. Who is being asked? About what? How?

Take the time to use Lodge's three questions to reflect on student involvement in governance at your institution.

3. What are the central and peripheral student self-governance structures on your campus?
4. How do you believe students on your campus view the student self-governance structures? What leads you to this belief?
5. What are the three most important questions currently being considered through shared governance at your institution? What role, if any, are students playing in those deliberations?
6. What incentives or reasons are there at your institution for students to take on roles in shared governance? What barriers are there? How might you help spread the word about the incentives and opportunities, and how might you help reduce the barriers?

Chapter 5

INTERSECTIONS OF LAW AND SHARED GOVERNANCE

From a legal perspective, concepts of shared governance reflect delegation from a college or university's governing board to share, to delegate, some its legal decision-making authority over institutional matters. As covered in Chapter One, such delegation can be based on democratic impulses and from an aim to guide particular institutional decisions based on academic and professional expertise. For purposes of this chapter, it is important to recognize the legal primacy of boards in institutional matters and their authority in relation to institutional control and decision-making.

While governing boards are recognized as possessing ultimate legal control over many aspects of institutional life, colleges and universities must also comply with an array of legal standards and obligations, including the need to navigate potential sources of legal liability that come with the legal rules to which higher education institutions are held accountable. University legal counsel are an important source of guidance and information in helping institutions to meet their legal obligations, but, in numerous instances, the knowledge and professional expertise of student affairs professionals are key in crafting student-centered responses, even as institutions navigate and respond to potential legal issues on campus.

Even while helping to ensure that institutional responses to legal issues encompass more than an overly narrow focus on legal compliance or risk management, part of the professional toolbox of student affairs professionals is having sufficient legal knowledge in particular areas to help guide and inform campus decision-making when legal considerations arise. As noted by one commentator—a former college president and state attorney general—the "nonlawyers on your staff must be well versed in higher education law" (Kroger, 2020). According to Kroger (2020), "In the best of possible worlds, your staff will know the law well enough to stay within well-established legal boundaries in their routine work and to recognize, in unusual situations, whether a potential legal issue exists or not, so they can consult with counsel when it is necessary." As part of his advice, Kroger (2020) also states that along with institutional legal counsel, staff need to be able to spot potential "legal disasters."

Rather than coming from an alarmist or overly legalistic orientation, the goal of this chapter is not to stir undue apprehension or to prompt student affairs professionals to operate only from a legal risk avoidance perspective that crowds out their roles as educators in serving students. Instead, a key aim of the chapter is to provide context and background for student affairs professionals to be able to better integrate legal knowledge and understanding with the other domains of professional expertise and experience that guide their work. To this end, the chapter provides a basic framework for sources of legal authority that often are applicable to colleges and universities. It also gives an overview of court systems and administrative bodies—such as the U.S. Department of Education and labor agencies like the National Labor Relations Board—external to campus that have legal authority over institutions in relation to particular areas.

Along with legal standards, the chapter also offers thoughts on the layered ways in which student affairs professionals respond to legal issues on campus. One layer, already described, involves how to ensure that individuals, in their professional positions, carry out relevant legal obligations and institutional standards and directives through having sufficient legal knowledge. Another layer deals with responding to situations that may involve legal ambiguity or uncertainty and when multiple campus players come together to assess a particular situation. In such instances, student affairs professional benefit from an understanding of the different kinds of perspectives that other professionals may bring to specific situations, such as, and notably, campus legal counsel.

As pointed out, the purpose of the chapter is not to cause apprehension or have student affairs professionals retreat from their ethical and professional obligations. Instead, the authors want to provide information for student affairs professionals to be better prepared to deal with legal concerns in ways that allow them to bring their talents, energy, and professional knowledge front and center in how campuses achieve legal compliance and minimize legal risk, but in ways that do not diminish or dehumanize our responsibilities to students and other members of campus. Such efforts may not always be easy, especially as campus legal obligations are numerous and often multifaceted and individuals are often willing to turn to the courts to resolve disputes. But, keeping focused on the primary role of student affairs professionals as educators and champions of students–as opposed to quasi-attorneys–is imperative in preserving the affirming and essential role that student affairs should have in the lives of students and in how our institutions operate in better and more equitable ways.

In terms of structure, the chapter first considers the sources of laws that provide the legal framework for institutional governance and also serve to define the legal obligations of colleges and universities. Next, as covered in the chapter, designation as a public or private college or university can have important consequences for governance and for the legal duties owed by institutions, namely in the area of constitutional protections provided by the Bill of Rights, such as those related to freedom of speech and religion. The chapter also considers the role of accrediting bodies in the regulation of higher education.

SOURCES OF LAW

There are several sources of law which can inform student affairs professional practice. Among these are constitutions, statutes, administrative agencies, court systems, and common law (particularly as it relates to torts and contracts). Each of these is described in this section.

Constitutions

At the apex of sources of law are the federal constitution and state constitutions. As King and Leuzinger (2015) state, "[c]onstitutions are authoritative texts that have legal force and prescribe principles of government" (p. 2). In general, constitutions are general documents "designed to be overarching frameworks to be interpreted by politicians and judges" (King & Leuzinger, 2015, p. 3). While the U.S. Constitution is relatively brief–with around 4,400 words–some states, like Texas and Alabama, are much longer and can be more prescriptive (King & Leuzinger, 2015). In the United States, the federal constitution is the supreme source of legal authority, including relation to state laws or even state constitutional provisions:

> No other law, either state or federal, may conflict with its provisions. Thus, although a state constitution is the highest state law authority, and state statutes and other state laws must be consistent with it, any of its provisions that conflict with the federal Constitution will be subject to invalidation by the courts. It is not considered a conflict, however, if state constitutions establish more expansive individual rights than those guaranteed by parallel provisions of the federal Constitution. (Kaplin, Lee, Hutchens, & Rooksby, 2019, p. 35)

The federal constitution does not contain specific provisions that relate to education. Outside of specialized institutions–including the military academies, degree programs operated by the department of defense, the sponsorship of Reserve Officers Training Corps (ROTC) programs at many institutions, and two postsecondary institutions that primarily serve American Indians–the federal government does not control, authorize, or operate postsecondary institutions (Kaplin et al., 2019, p. 32). However, the federal government and federal law have increasingly come to exercise an important role in how colleges and universities operate. As discussed later in the chapter, a key area of federal involvement has come from the individual rights provided through the federal constitution–such as freedom of speech and religion and due process rights–and applicable to students and employees at public colleges and universities. While not a direct form of legal oversight, the federal government also has imposed duties on colleges and universities in exchange for institutions or students to be eligible to receive sources of federal funding, such as grants or federal financial aid loans made and guaranteed by the federal government. The federal government can also regulate higher education when Congress exercises its constitutional powers, such as in matters related to commerce, immigration, or employment.

While the role of the federal government and federal law continues to play an increasing role in higher education, state law, including state constitutional provisions, have traditionally played the role of "primary external 'governors' of higher education, at least in terms of legal theory" (Kaplin et al., 2019, p. 30). Whereas the federal government is a government of limited powers, state governments, in contrast, are

> [G]overnments of general powers that typically have express authority over education built into their state constitutions. They have plenary authority to create, organize, support, and dissolve public educational institutions ... and they have general police powers under which they charter and license private higher education institution and recognize their authority to grant degrees.... States also authorize out-of-state institutions to offer courses or degree programs to residents in the state. (Kaplin et al., 2019, p. 30)

In contrast to the federal constitution, many state constitutions have provisions that establish one or more public colleges or higher education systems. Thus, alongside authorizing and regulating private higher education providers, the states also have legal authority for public colleges and university that fall under some form of state or public control for purposes of governance. While constitutional provisions often vest state legislators with the authority to define the powers and authorities of the governing boards of these public institutions, a select number of states provide some level of constitutionally protected institutional autonomy to governing boards, what has been referred to as "constitutional autonomy." California, Michigan, and Minnesota are three primary examples of states that grant such constitutional autonomy to one or more institutions in their respective states (Hutchens, 2009). In California, for instance, the University of California (UC) Board of Regents is a constitutionally empowered governing board for the ten campuses that comprise the UC system. In contrast the California State University System and its twenty-three campuses are governed by a board of trustees that has its powers and duties delegated to it by the California legislature. In Michigan, governing boards for multiple universities in the state have constitutionally protected authority. Especially in California and Michigan, state courts have handed down legal opinions recognizing important constitutional authority for these constitutionally empowered governing boards. For example, in a 2000 legal opinion, a California appeals court stated that the rules and policies of the California regents had a status similar to legislative statutes for the purposes of judicial interpretation (*Kim v. Regents,* 2000; see also Hutchens, 2009).

While constitutions stand as controlling sources of law in how specific institutions and college and university systems are authorized and/or organized, constitutional provisions are often only a starting point for legal authority and issues related to higher education. For specific legal standards and responsibilities related to higher education, we turn to sources that include statutes (laws passed by the U.S. Congress or state legislatures), rules and guidance from administrative agencies delegated the authority to enforce and interpret statutory provisions, and rulings from state and federal courts.

Statutes

A key source of law comes in the form of statutes passed by the U.S. Congress and state legislatures. Additionally, similar provisions, ordinances, can be passed by local governmental bodies such as county and city governments (Kaplin et al., 2019). Federal laws and local ordinances can be specific to colleges and universities, but the "greatest amount of [laws aimed at postsecondary education] is written by the states. Examples include laws establishing and regulating state postsecondary institutions or systems, laws creating statewide coordinating councils for postsecondary education, and laws providing for the licensure of postsecondary institutions" (Kaplin et al., 2019, p. 36).

Besides laws that are specific to higher education, colleges and universities are subject to multiple state and federal laws of general application. For example, as with other private and public employers, both public and private colleges and universities are subject to various state and federal laws that prohibit discrimination in employment, such as on the basis of age, race, or sexual orientation. Federal and state laws are collected and arranged (codified), both in print and online. For instance, most federal statutes are contained in the *United States Code* or the *United States Code Annotated* (Kaplin et al., 2019). There are also parallel works in which state laws are collected and arranged.

As covered, statutes, especially those at the state level, often provide the key source of language for setting out standards for the authorization of higher education institutions to operate and, for public colleges and universities, the structure and authorities of governing boards with oversight of public higher education systems or institutions. Statutes, from both the federal and state governments, also set out many of the legal duties that colleges and universities must adhere to, such as ones related to discrimination in learning and work environments. Some statutes can have special application for public colleges and universities. Examples include state laws dealing with open records or meetings–sometimes called "sunshine" laws, statutes that guide the procedures that state agencies, including public colleges and universities, must following in the purchasing of goods and services, and legal provisions related to hiring.

As with constitutional provisions, laws often require further interpretation or elaboration to comply with or implement statutory requirements. Such statutory "gap-filling" if often carried out by administrative agencies with authority to enforce particular statutory provisions. At the federal level, for example, when an agency has appropriately exercised it rulemaking authority, the agency's interpretation of a law under its regulatory authority receives substantial deference from courts. Courts also serve an important role in interpreting laws and legal provisions alongside, including ensuring that administrative agencies have acted within the appropriate scope of their authority. Courts also serve an important role in making sure that laws and the actions of officials are permissible under applicable laws and constitutional provisions. As covered, state courts also play an important role in defining the legal duties imposed on colleges and universities in the area known as tort law, which is also discussed. Administrative agencies and courts and the roles that each play is considered next.

Administrative Agencies

An important source of legal authority impacting colleges and universities comes from state and federal administrative agencies that are responsible for enforcing and implementing particular statutes. As discussed in Chapter Two, administrative agencies, such as the U.S. Department of Education, issue rules and regulations that interpret and guide entities subject to particular laws, including colleges and universities, on how to comply with statutory requirements. Extended attention is given to the role of agencies in Chapter Six, which covers policy and policymaking. As long as rules or regulations are crafted so as to stay within the purview of the pertinent statute and conform to applicable procedures required in creating rules or regulations, such as giving appropriate notice to the public of proposed rulemaking and obtaining public comment, agency rules and regulations and their interpretation of the statute at issue typically receive substantial deference from courts. Final federal regulations are collected and organized in the Code of Federal Regulations after they have been published in the Federal Registrar (Kaplin et al., 2019). Some states also have similar publications or ways for organizing the regulations of state administrative agencies. As covered in Chapter Six, administrative agencies also issue documents—such as Dear Colleague Letters—that are not an exercise in formal rulemaking but that can help provide guidance on the agency's interpretation of a statute and accompanying legal standards.

Administrative agencies can also act in quasi-judicial capacities in carrying out their functions. For instance, the U.S. Department of Education may hold administrative hearings to consider when institutions have violated federal financial aid provisions, such that students at an institution are ineligible to participate in federal financial aid programs. The Office for Civil Rights (OCR) of the Department of Education conducts investigations for potential violations of multiple civil rights laws. If the OCR concludes that a violation has occurred, it attempts to negotiate a resolution with the institution. If these voluntary efforts are not successful, the OCR may initiate proceedings to discontinue a recipient's eligibility for its students to receive federal funds. It may also refer issue to the Department of Justice (U.S. Department of Education, n.d.)

The National Labor Relations Board (NLRB) provides another example of a federal agency, one that decides issues often relevant for higher education and that exercises quasi-judicial functions. Under the National Labor Relations Act (NLRA), collective bargaining rights for employees at private colleges and universities fall under the authority of the National Labor Relations Board. The collective bargaining rights of employees at public higher institutions are subject to state law. The NLRB has primarily carried out its role to interpret and carry out the provisions of the NLRA through in its quasi-judicial capacity and the settling of collective bargaining disputes. For example, putting aside the decision of a regional director, the NLRB declined to assert jurisdiction to determine whether scholarship football players at a private university should be classified as employees for purposes on the NLRA. The Board has also issued a series of contrasting decisions—based on the political makeup of Board membership—regarding whether graduate student employees at private colleges and universities should be eligible to engage in unionizing activities (Flaherty, 2019). While it has used its formal rule-making authority less than other agencies–relying instead on its quasi-judicial authority to decide issues involving the NLRA on a case-by-case basis–the NLRB can engage in rule making. For example, it has proposed a rule that would make graduate students ineligible to be classified as employees under the NLRA for purposes of collective bargaining activities protected under the act. See Chapter Six for more the role of administrative agencies and how they function.

Court Systems

The United States has a system of federal courts and state courts. State courts hear cases dealing with matters of state law, but they are also able to decide issues that involve federal legal standards. For instance, a student suing an institution and individual employees could bring federal constitutional claims, such as ones based on First Amendment rights, or federal statutory \different ways. One or more types of courts serve as trial courts and are often the initial court to hear legal arguments. Then, there are appellate courts that hear appeals from lower courts. Some states have intermediate appeals courts that take cases, and then cases can be reviewed by the state's supreme court. Some states have separate appeals court to hear criminal cases and civil cases. Some ten states do not have intermediate appeals courts (see National Center for State Courts, n.d.). States also have specialized courts, such as family courts or courts that handle juvenile justice matters. The National Center for State Courts has useful resources and information that allow users to compare and contrast the courts in each state and to learn about the different types of courts in each state and the various cases handled by particular courts.

Common Law–Torts and Contracts

In some instances, state courts may decide legal disputes that are not based on a specific statute or agency rule. In doing so, courts engage in what is commonly referred to the making of "American common law" (Kaplin et al., 2019, p. 38). Two areas of common law informing state courts that are especially relevant for colleges and universities are in the areas of contracts and tort law. The role of common law in federal court decisions is a more limited and murky matter.

Torts

A *tort* is "broadly defined as a civil wrong" committed by an individual or an institution, which can include a college or university, for which courts can provide a remedy, such as monetary damages (Kaplin et al., 2019, p. 228). Among the various types of torts, negligence claims are some of most common that can arise in litigation involving higher education. A negligence claim is based on (1) some type of duty was owed to an individual, such as a student, by an individual or institution, which can include a college or university, (2) the duty was broken (breached), and (3) this breach was the legal cause of injury or harm to the individual. The contours of tort law, including negligence claims, have been developed through cases decided by state courts. While the general standards of negligence and other torts are often similar across states, variations exist in how the courts of particular states interpret tort standards, including whether a particular tort is recognized by a state's courts. The law of torts, especially particular torts such as negligence, provides an additional important source of law for higher education. Institutions or their employees that fail to fulfill their legal duties in particular instances can be subject to legal responsibility and liability. While an important source of legal duty, public colleges and universities may have some immunities available to lawsuits under principles of what are known as sovereign immunity. Public, non-profit institutions may also have some defenses available as charitable organizations. Despite the availability of immunity from suit in some situations, tort standards are an important source of law for higher education.

Contracts

Another important source of law and legal obligations for colleges and universities comes from contract law (Kaplin et al., 2019). For example, to varying and contrasting degrees, courts have looked to contract principles in as defining the general legal relationship between a college or university and its students. While there are some specific types of contractual arrangements that can exist between institutions and students, such as one for housing or meal plans, courts in many states also look to contract principles in addressing legal claims by students in areas such as academic decisions and student conduct. Rather than a specific document, in these instances, courts often look to multiple sources, such as handbooks, catalogues, and course syllabi. As with tort standards, contract law has been a creature of state law. As such, while important characteristics are shared in contract law standards across states, there can be important nuances in how the courts of specific states interpret contract standards, including in the area of the student-institutional relationship in higher education. In fact, some state courts have been reluctant to categorize this relationship as primarily contractual in nature for purposes of law. However, state courts, even ones not explicitly framing the student-institutional relationship as one primarily contractual in nature, often turn to contract principles and standards in settling legal disputes between colleges and students.

Federal Common Law

The concept of a federal common law has a more uncertain place in American jurisprudence than that of state courts. In general, the idea of federal common law as applied to federal legal standards is more restricted than that of common law areas, such as torts and contract, developed by state courts. The view is that federal courts, when considering matters of federal law, should look to standards based on statutes or the constitution or interpretations of federal statutes developed by administrative agencies. This does not mean that courts, when interpreting federal statutes and constitutional provisions, are not engaged in important "gap filling" and interpretive roles when it comes to interpreting federal legal standards. Often, statutory language or administrative guidance may not answer a particular question presented to a court. A recent example of such an issue has involved the application of protections under Title IX to students based on transgender status. In the absence of clear statutory language or federal rules or guidance, courts have had to determine the statute's applicability to discrimination claims based on transgender status or sexual orientation. In essence, courts have had to consider whether such forms of discrimination are on the basis of sex for purposes of Title IX. Similar questions have arisen for employment law under Title VII. At the time of the publication of this book, the U.S. Supreme Court had decided to review three cases involving whether Title VII applies to discrimination on the basis of sexual orientation or transgender status (Hurley, 2019). The outcome in these cases, along with affecting employment practices in higher education, will likely also be important in how courts interpret these issues for purposes of Title IX.

Depending on how courts rule in interpreting a statue, Congress, at times, will occasionally amend federal law in response to how courts have interpreted particularly statutory requirements. For example, Congress has previously amended or enacted new civil rights laws to undo legal interpretations from the U.S. Supreme Court. Congress passed the Civil Rights Restoration Act in 1987 in response to a U.S. Supreme Court case, *Grove City College v. Bell* (1984), in which the Court ruled that only the specific parts of a college program or activity receiving federal aid were subject to federal civil rights laws (Devins, 2008). Under the Civil Rights Restoration Act, Congress, which also overrode a veto of the legislation by President Ronald Reagan in enacting the law, made coverage of federal civil rights laws such as Title IX apply to all programs and activities at educational institutions, even if a program or activity did not receive federal funds. The case and subsequent change in law provide a higher education-specific example of how Congress can potentially respond to interpretations of federal statutes by the U.S. Supreme Court–or other federal courts–that run counter to congressional sentiment and intent. While Congress can step in, as it did after *Grove City College,* the interpretations given by the U.S. Supreme Court and lower courts to matters of federal statutory law are often left in place, as changes to law can be difficult to enact. As such, like administrative agencies, courts also often play an important role in interpreting federal statutes, dealing with issues not explicitly covered under statutory provisions or in rules or regulations issued by agencies.

In terms of state common law, federal courts also can decide issues of state law, including those based on the common law of a particular state. For example, a student who is a legal resident from one state and attends a college or university in another state may rely on what is called diversity jurisdiction to have a suit against the institution heard in federal court on the basis of what is known as diversity jurisdiction, as long as the appropriate conditions are satisfied for diversity jurisdiction to exist. When a federal court hears a case based on diversity jurisdiction, it is applying the applicable state law and legal standards at issue, those developed under common law principles in state courts.

Both state and federal courts serve as important sources of law for legal standards to which colleges and universities must adhere. The common law produced by state courts provide important legal obligations for colleges and universities, such as in the area of tort and contract law. Another important function relates to the role of courts in interpreting statutory and constitutional provisions. While legislative bodies can amend statutes in response to the interpretation of a statute, courts play the primary role in the interpretation of constitutional standards, whether the courts of a state or the federal courts. State laws (including state constitutional provisions) cannot preempt or override valid exercises of federal law, and neither federal nor state laws can infringe on federal constitutional standards. In this interpretive dynamic, the U.S. Supreme Court stands as the final legal arbiter of whether a state action encroaches on federal authority or the federal constitution or when a federal legislative enactment or action is impermissible based on the federal constitution.

PUBLIC VERSUS PRIVATE

In terms of important context for issues related to governance, an important legal distinction in American higher education is the one between public and private colleges and universities. From a governance and law perspective, a significant distinction between public and private is that the governing entity for public colleges and universities rests, in one form or another, with the state government in which the institution is located. States organize the governance for the colleges and universities under their control in different ways. For example, some states place control of all four-year public colleges and universities in the state under the control of single governing board. Likewise, a state may create a single governing board to govern its public community colleges. Other states have a more dispersed system of governance for public institutions, where separate governing boards have control over one or more public colleges or universities in the state. In a small number of states–as discussed previously in the chapter–constitutional provisions establish the governing authorities for the governing boards of one or more institutions. For instance, Michigan has granted constitutional authority to governing boards for its public universities. When exercising their constitutional powers in an appropriate manner, these governing boards may not have their authority abridged by state government. For most states, however, a state legislature possesses ultimate legal authority over its public colleges and universities. It then has delegated this authority to one or more governing boards for public institutions in the state. In some states, the constitution may stipulate that a governing board exists, but then it often leaves it to the state legislature to define the extent of the board's powers.

Legal control over private colleges and universities is vested in governing entities that are not under the control of state government. An important episode in the development of private higher education in the United States came with the *Dartmouth College* case (Thelin, 2019). In this historic case, the U.S. Supreme Court invalidated an effort by the New Hampshire legislature to overturn a charter and reconstitute the governing board of Dartmouth College. While not occurring immediately, the case would help to lay the foundation for a system of private and public higher education in the United States. Other developments, such as the institutions that came into being under the Morrill Land-Grant Acts would also spur development of public and private colleges and universities (Thelin, 2019). For non-profit private institutions, they typically have a board that has extensive legal authority over the institution. For religiously affiliated institutions, a religious authority may also exercise some degree of governing authority over the college or university. For-profit colleges may be authorized or licensed under different state procedures than those for non-profit private institutions. In terms of governance, for-profit institutions can be arranged in a corporate structure, with a board having fiduciary duties to the shareholders who hold stock in the company that owns the institution. Especially for a smaller for-profit institution, ownership of the company may be privately held and owned by a smaller group of individuals.

Status as a private college or university is often important in the legal realm in terms of what is known as the "state action" doctrine (Kaplin et al., 2019). The liberties granted under the constitution's Bill of Rights apply to governmental actors at the state and federal levels. For instance, rights of free speech and religion, due process, and privacy cannot be improperly abridged by governmental actors, including those at public colleges and universities. In contrast, these constitutional protections do not apply to private actors. Thus, a private college or university is not required to afford its students or employees First Amendment speech rights. A religious institution can also require students and employees to adhere to certain religious tenants as a condition of enrollment or employment. Status as non-state actor gives private colleges and universities considerable legal discretion in defining their institutional missions and authority over students and employees that can be distinct from their public higher education counterparts.

The fact that private higher education institutions are not held to the individual constitutional protections found in the Bill of Rights does not make them immune to state and federal legal authority in numerous areas. Just as with other private actors, state and federal laws can still regulate a host of items at private institutions, such as those related to health and safety, discrimination in employment, or discrimination on the basis of disability. For the federal government, just as it does with public colleges and universities, private institutions must comply with various standards to be eligible to participate in multiple federal funding programs, such those tied to financial aid for students or research grant programs. FERPA and Title IX are two well-known examples of statues that place requirements on institutions in exchange for eligibility for institutions or students to be able to participate in federal funding programs. Private higher education providers also may not have the governmental immunities available to public institutions, which may increase their legal liability in certain situations, such as issues related to tort liability.

ACCREDITATION

Considerations of governance and law are also informed by taking the role of accreditation into account. Accreditors are non-governmental actors that play an important part in U.S. higher education. A key function of accreditors, one empowered to them by the federal government, is to authorize that an institution's offerings are of sufficient quality to be able for students to participate in federal financial aid program (Kaplin et al., 2019). As many colleges and universities are strongly dependent on students being able to access federal loans and grants, this makes the role of institutional accreditation an especially important one. Under the current accreditation system, there exists a system of regional accrediting bodies that accredit institutions based on geographic region, though recent regulatory changes will allow regional accreditors to operate outside of their traditional geographic area (Kaplin et al., 2019). While regional accreditors have focused on public and non-for-profit private colleges and universities, the federal government has also recognized national accrediting bodies that have tended to serve the for-profit sector.

In considering accreditation, it is important to distinguish between institutional accreditation and types of specialized accreditation that focus on particular academic programs. These types of programmatic accreditation can often be important for professional licensure. For example, teacher accreditation programs are often required to be accredited by an organization approved by the state so that graduates of the program are eligible for teacher licensure. Counselor education programs are another example of a type of program that generally must receive programmatic accreditation for its graduates to be eligible for professional licensure. Law schools provide another example, as states often require future lawyers to have attended a law school that is accredited by the American Bar Association.

Accreditation at the institutional level or programmatic level is relevant to governance considerations because of the limits placed on colleges and universities and their governing boards. A governing board that runs afoul of accreditation standards can imperil the ability of students to participate in federal financial aid programs. Lack of accreditation can also impair the ability of its students and graduates to transfer credit or be eligible to enroll in graduate or professional programs at other institutions. The loss of programmatic accreditation can make an institution's graduate ineligible for professional licensure. Accrediting bodies do not possess formal authority over institutional governance or the type of legal power held by courts, but they exert a substantial influence over how institutions operate and the ways in which they are governed.

CONCLUSION

As covered in this chapter, multiple sources account for the legal standards and obligations to which colleges and institutions adhere to. From a governance perspective, sources of law and legal standards exert a notable external influence on how colleges and universities operate. For public institutions, state constitutional and statutory language can empower a govern board or establish the framework of institutional governance, with the composition, duties, and authority of the governing board defined by legislative enactment. Private institutions, at a minimum, need legal authorization to operate in a state. While not directly influencing governance, standards imposed by laws, constitutional provisions, or agency rulemaking or decision-making also place important constraints on how institutions operate. Colleges and universities, both public and private, have to comply with legal standards specifically aimed at higher education institutions and general laws and legal standards that are also applicable to institutions. Alongside mandatory legal obligations, institutions also "voluntarily" adhere to legal or regulatory standards or rules established by accrediting bodies to be eligible for governmental funding directly or for their students to be eligible for funding or licensure. Legal standards, even when indirect, exert an pervasive and significant influence on governance in higher education.

REFLECTION QUESTIONS

1. Using a 4-point scale where 4 is fully informed and 1 is fully uninformed, how would you assess your knowledge about areas of the law and sources of law prior to beginning to read this book? Where does that knowledge come from (e.g., graduate program, experience as a student, or experience as a higher education faculty member or administrative staff member)?
2. Thinking about the sources of law identified in the chapter, are there areas which have a particularly strong impact? If so, how do you and your colleagues keep informed about decisions from that source of law? How are discussions regarding compliance handled on your campus?
3. Is the institution at which you serve public or private? How does that source of control play itself out in shared governance practices and structures on your campus?
4. What comments about shared governance, if any, appeared in the most recent accreditation report for your college or university? Do you feel those comments were thorough and an accurate reflection of the reality of shared governance as you see it at your institution?

5. What new information or insights about areas and sources of the law, if any, did you gain from reading this chapter, and how will you use the newfound information and insights moving forward to enhance your professional performance and development?

Chapter 6

THE INDIVIDUAL VOICE IN SHARED GOVERNANCE: INSTITUTIONAL ACTOR VERSUS PRIVATE CITIZEN

Student affairs professionals, like other members of the campus community, looking to participate in the life of an institution through its shared governance procedures can be left to balance competing, and, at times, conflicting, demands. One challenge that student affairs professionals may face is balancing their roles as agents or officers of the institution versus their roles as private citizens. With an increased emphasis on campus activism and pushing institutions to live up to aspirations expressed in institutional missions and creeds and to respond to instances of discrimination or oppression, student affairs professional may feel a tension between carrying out their professional duties and representing the institution and advocating for their personal beliefs and assessments of institutional performance. This chapter considers some of the types of issues that can arise as individuals work to balance their roles as employees and that as a private citizen in society and on campus.

LEGAL STANDARDS GOVERNING EMPLOYEE, STUDENT SPEECH RIGHTS

This section considers the legal rights that can apply to employee speech in colleges and universities, including in terms of participation in shared governance matters. The section is important to this book because those working at colleges and universities have to navigate environments in which they may be viewed as speaking for the institution and other instances when they may be seeking to inject their personal ideas and views into governance related matters. At times, issues on campus can become heated, and senior leaders and members of governing boards can be subject to intense criticism. For example, at the authors' own institution, strong debates have arisen over the continuing presence on campus of a Confederate memorial (Ganucheau, 2020). Our university is, of course, not alone in the presence of contentious issues on campus–such as those involving issues of racism, and social justice–that can engender strong debate and, at times, campus protests. In such a context, university employees can be caught in tensions around meaningful (or not) opportunities for participation in shared governance, the responsibility to act as an official or agent in carrying out or communicating institutional prerogatives on matters, and deciding when it is appropriate as a private individual to voice disagreement with institutional decisions or actions. Deciding which speaker's hat to wear–that of employee or private citizen–in particular instances has important connections in relation to how individuals on campus have to switch between speaking for themselves, including from a shared governance perspective, and speaking for or representing the institution in an employee capacity.

Free Speech on Campus

As covered in Chapter Five, private colleges and universities are not bound by the constitutional liberties found in the Bill of Rights. As such, a private higher education institution is not held to the First Amendment when it comes to speech rights for students, staff, and faculty. Private institutions may voluntarily adopt comparable speech rights, such as is the case for when a private college or university adopts tenure protections and academic freedom standards of the AAUP. In such instances, faculty speech rights, including participation in shared governance, may be protected under principles of contract law. Similarly, student or employee handbooks may lay out speech protections that are potentially enforceable through contract law and that apply to contexts involving shared governance. But, a private college or university is not required to provide such speech protections, including as a way promote open discourse in matters related to shared governance.

Student Speech

In the case of student speech, California has enacted a law that provides a notable exception for student speech protections in private higher education. Under what is known as the Leonard Law, private, secular colleges and universities in the state must afford students the same speech rights as provided under the First Amendment to their student peers at public higher education institutions (Kaplin et al., 2019, p. 1319). Outside of such an exception as that found in California, however, private higher education institutions are not legally required to do so but may voluntarily grant speech freedoms to students, staff, and faculty. Some private institutions place limitations on speech that would not be permitted at public institution. For example, some private, religious colleges require members of the campus community, including employees, to adhere to a statement of faith. Or, while the First Amendment may protect speech that is hateful or detestable, whether from students and employees, private colleges and universities are able to enact standards that would likely run afoul of First Amendment speech standards if enacted at a public institution. While many private higher education institutions have adopted similar speech protections as exist at public colleges and universities under the First Amendment, such an approach is not universal.

While not subject to First Amendment requirements, several important legal exceptions to institutional authority related to the regulation of speech exist for private colleges and universities. For instance, the reporting of civil rights violations, such as laws pertaining to discrimination based on race or sex, can be protected against retaliation (Kaplin et al., 2019). For another example, under labor law, speech and communications related to lawful and permitted unionizing activity is also protected (Kaplin et al., 2019). Outside of such specific legal requirements that may provide speech protections not grounded in the First Amendment, however, it largely rests with the governing authority of a private college or university to set the parameters of free speech rights on campus, including in the context of shared governance.

In the case of a public college or university, First Amendment speech protections apply to faculty, staff, or student speech, though the contours of speech rights available in a particular situation are dependent upon multiple factors, which can include status as an employee or student. In terms of shared governance and offering views on institutional affairs, students at public higher education institutions possess expansive speech rights. Student speech can be more subject to educator control when it takes place in an instructional setting, but such educator authority typically would not apply in terms of participation in shared governance matters. Outside of teaching contexts, an institution may impose reasonable restrictions on speech and expression, such as on time, place, and manner to ensure smooth institutional operations and safety. Officials, however, cannot suppress student speech because of its content outside of special circumstances, such as speech that constitutes discrimination under law or a direct threat to others (Kaplin, Lee, Hutchens, & Rooksby, 2019). As an example, if students are displeased with institutional actions, senior leaders, or governing board members, they are well within their constitutional rights to speak out, to engage in lawful protest, and to advocate for change on campus, including on issues related to governance. Institutional leaders' mere displeasure with students' views or speech does not constitute a reason to suppress student speech (see e.g., LaBanc, Fernandez, Hutchens, & Melear, 2020; Sun & McClellan, 2020).

Important caveats exist on student speech rights in public higher education. Many students, both graduate and undergraduate, also work in employee capacities on campus or may take on service roles, such as serving as program or institutional ambassadors. In carrying out these kinds of duties, the student speech may be categorized for legal purposes as more akin to employee speech than student speech. As covered immediately below, when engaged in speech as an employee, an institution may be able to assert substantial control over the speech. Speech issues related to college athletes have also raised important speech considerations. From one perspective, previous legal cases establish that college athletes, as students, should possess broad speech protections, such as for protest activities, including those associated with sporting events, such as kneeling during the national anthem to protest racism and injustice (Bentley, 2016). In contrast, another view is that participation in sports is voluntary and that public institutions should be able to regulate college athletes' speech as part of the scholarship agreement, with the view that athletes' speech should be analyzed by courts under the same or similar standards applied to speech by public employees (Penrose, 2014).

Employee Speech

Unlike the expansive rights that can apply to student speech outside of an instructional context and not violative of other lawful speech prohibitions, public colleges and universities are often afforded substantial legal latitude in regulating employee speech. While subject to critique, the U.S. Supreme Court has developed a set of legal standards that significantly curtail the First Amendment speech rights of employees in public colleges and universities when they are engaged in carrying out their official job duties. In *Garcetti v. Ceballos* (2006), the Supreme Court decided a case that involved a deputy district attorney, Richard Ceballos, for Los Angeles County who claimed that he was retaliated against for a memorandum in which he concluded that police officers had made misrepresentations in statements in an affidavit used to obtain a search warrant. A federal appeals court decided that the retaliation claimed by Ceballos violated his First Amendment speech rights. Reversing this decision, the Supreme Court, in a 5–4 decision, held that Ceballos' speech was not protected by the First Amendment.

In the *Garcetti* case, The Supreme Court laid out a bright-line rule for employee speech and the First Amendment, holding that when an employee engages in speech as part of carrying out their official duties, the speech does not qualify for First Amendment protection. The Court noted that an employee might be able to raise another type of legal claim for being retaliated against for their speech, such as protections found in state Whistleblower laws, but could not look to the First Amendment. Under *Garcetti,* then, when a public employee, including in public higher education, engages in speech as part of carrying out their official employment duties, the speech is unprotected by the First Amendment.

What about the private speech of an employee at a public college or university? In Garcetti and previous cases, the Supreme Court outlined standards for when private employee speech could be protected by the first Amendment based on whether the speech at issue deals with matters of public or private concern. If the speech at issue only deals with a matter of private concern, the Court has held that such speech is not shielded by the First Amendment when action is taken by an employer for the speech. For example, in *Connick v. Myers* (1983), the Supreme Court held that an assistant district attorney distributing a questionnaire to other employees about office management by the district attorney only dealt with matters of private concern. Thus, the assistant district attorney's speech under consideration in the case was not subject to First Amendment protection.

A topic that was raised but left unresolved in *Garcetti* dealt with the issue of faculty speech and academic freedom. Justice David Souter, in a dissenting opinion, raised academic freedom concerns if the standard announced in *Garcetti* was applied to speech by faculty members in public higher education that involved their research. Writing for the majority, Justice Anthony Kennedy stated that Justice Souter raised a potentially important question but not one before the Supreme Court in *Garcetti.* Since the Garcetti decision, some courts have concluded that faculty members at public colleges and universities continue to possess First Amendment rights related to their scholarship, teaching, and participation in shared governance (e.g., *Demers v. Austin,* 2014). In contrast, other courts have decided that the standard announced in *Garcetti* applies to faculty speech made as part of professors carrying out their employment duties, included those related to research, teaching, and service and participation in governance matters (Kaplin et al., 2019).

Even as courts continue to wrestle with whether *Garcetti* applies to faculty professional speech related to carrying out employment duties, courts have consistently ruled, on the basis of *Garcetti,* that speech made by staff in carrying out their employment duties is excluded from First Amendment protection. For example, a federal appeals court looked to *Garcetti* in denying a First Amendment retaliation claim by five staff members of a university counseling center who had submitted a memorandum to university leadership that was critical of the center's director (*Alves v. Board of Regents of the University System of Georgia,* 2015). In the memorandum, the counseling center employees alleged that the center director had engaged in mismanagement and leadership lapses that threatened the center's reputation and potentially had a negative impact on client care. The appeals court held that even if the allegations by the former employees were true, they undertook to write the memorandum in "the course of carrying out their daily [employment] activities" (*Alves v. Board of Regents of the University System of Georgia,* 2015, p. 1165). Thus, as speech made in the course of carrying out job duties, it was ineligible for First Amendment protection.

The *Alves* case illustrates the sweeping nature of *Garcetti* when it comes to a lack of First Amendment speech rights for public higher education employees–including student affairs professionals–in carrying out their employment duties. If speech is classified to have taken place as part of carrying out employment duties, then it is ineligible for First Amendment protection. While some limits have been placed on *Garcetti,* such as a college employee receiving legal protection when giving truthful testimony to a court in a criminal case (see *Lane v. Franks,* 2014), cases such as *Alves* are notable in classifying employee speech as falling under the auspices of managerial control. *Garcetti* and subsequent cases raise important questions of what it means for shared governance when the speech of employees is viewed by courts as under institutional control and exempt from the First Amendment.

Employee, Public Concern, or Individual?

For public employee speech that takes place outside of carrying out employment duties, courts consider whether the speech deals with a matter of public or private concern, the issue raised in the *Connick v. Myers* case discussed previously in this section. If the speech is deemed to have involved matters of private concern, such as only involving internal employment grievances, then the employee's claim is blunted for First Amendment purposes. For example, in the *Alves* case covered earlier, a federal appeals court held, as an alternative ground for ruling against the employees, that a memorandum detailing concerns with how a university counseling center was being led dealt only with matters of private concern related to the center's operation and employment matters. The court noted that the memorandum represented an effort to use internal channels within the institution to communicate concerns. Thus, the court also precluded First Amendment for the employees' speech by categorizing it as only dealing with issues of private concern and not of interest to the general public.

If a public employee's speech is determined to deal with a matter of public concern and offered in an individual's capacity as a private citizen, then courts engage in a balancing test to determine whether the public employer can restrict the speech or take punitive action against the employee for the speech. The foundational public employee speech case, *Pickering v. Board of Education* (1968), involved the U.S.

Supreme Court upholding the right of a teacher to write a letter to a local newspaper critical of the local school board for the school district in which the teacher was employed.

In terms of the balancing process for private speech by a public employee, the more senior the position held by an employee can be a factor in tipping the balance in favor of the employer's interests to regulate the speech. In one illustrative case, a senior university administrator in human resources wrote a letter to a newspaper, in her capacity as a private citizen, that was critical of comparisons between civil rights efforts for LGBTQ individuals and the civil rights movement for African Americans (*Dixon v. University of Toledo,* 2012). The administrator claimed that she was improperly removed from her senior position in the university's human resources office because of the letter. A federal appeals court concluded that the university's interests outweighed those of the administrator to write the letter due to the individual's senior-level position and responsibility for oversight related to institutional non-discrimination policies, including those dealing with sexual orientation or identity.

Even as courts have tilted the legal scales in favor of managerial control when it comes to employee speech, individuals are left to consider how and when to convey their speech as private citizens, including on matters that touch on institutional governance. One consideration to keep in mind that as a person assumes more senior roles in the institution, their range of private speech rights may become more constricted from a First Amendment vantage, as highlighted in the case covered earlier. Institutional leaders and the governing board may point to the need to have its more senior administrators not in active opposition to decisions, policies, and communications that represent the official stances of the institution, and courts may likely be persuaded by such arguments. Likewise, even if not in a more senior position, the closer that an employee comments on matters involving their direct working environment or unit could override their First Amendment rights as a private citizen with the need for an institution to ensure the smooth functioning of its operations.

Importantly, even if engaged in private speech and not directly related to campus matters, institutional leaders or boards may react to calls to dismiss employees whose speech has displeased key stakeholders, such as state elected officials. For example, a dean of students at the University of Alabama resigned after the conservative media outlet Breitbart published a piece on tweets by the dean critical of police and racism in the United States (Johnson, 2019). The tweets were made prior to the individual becoming an employee at the University of Alabama. University officials did not fire the dean, but the Breitbart coverage of the tweets were clearly integral in the dean's separation from the institution.

At the authors' home institution, an incident occurred in which a professor's tweet critical of a call to show deference to senators by political commentator Joe Scarborough caught the attention of the university's former chancellor and governing board members (Amy, 2019). The professor's social media comments were clearly made in the context of speech as a private citizen and on extramural matters, that is external to issues involving the institution. Still, several members of the institution's governing board voted against granting the professor tenure. The incident, like that at the University of Alabama, highlights how imprudent actions by institutional leaders and governing board members can encroach on the speech rights of employees as private citizens. These types of actions can have an overall chilling effect on all types of speech by employees of the campus community, including in relation to governance matters.

Words of Advice and Encouragement

Our message for student affairs professionals is not a blanket one to be silent and to refrain from weighing in on institutional governance matters, or other matters of campus or societal importance. Rather, we think it is prudent for student affairs professionals to make informed decisions regarding when and how to use their voice as a private citizen in particular situations, including when the issue merits taking professional risk and "speaking up" and "speaking out." When choosing to speak as a private citizen, such as on social media or in a letter to the editor of a newspaper, student affairs professionals will want to be careful to note that they are speaking in a private, individual capacity and that they are not speaking for the institution or representing its views. Additionally, when engaged in such private citizen speech, individuals may likely want to refrain from using their official institution email accounts or even institutional resources, such as, for example, using work materials to make banners for a protest that concerns issues on campus or using institutional letterhead or copiers. Some institutions have also adopted social media policies, and individuals will want to understand the parameters set out in these policies, whether engaged in speech as a private citizen or as an institutional actor or representative. In fact, such policies may provide a useful shared governance context to help ensure that institutions do not seek to unduly control the private speech of employees, including in relation to matters of shared governance.

As individuals engage in the personal calculus of using their private citizen voice in shared governance, as noted, we are not advocating silence and acquiescence. Instead, we urge student affairs professionals to understand the policies, practices, and unique contexts of their institutions and to make informed choices about using their individual voice. At times, individuals may want to clearly delineate when speaking on behalf of the college or university and when expressing views in an individual capacity. As student affairs professionals make decisions about how and when to use their individual voices in shared governance matters, we also contend that those professionals with the privilege of being more able to raise their voices than others on campus have an ethical and professional responsibility to advocate for their peers and students in shared governance matters and to push institutional actions to match institutional rhetoric when it comes to matters of equity, inclusion, and social justice.

FLIPPING DEBATES ON SPEECH FREEDOMS IN SHARED GOVERNANCE

Alongside the considerations that individual professionals must make in response to factors that include their professional positions and the campus culture around issues of speech, institutions should also consider the extent to which policies and practices support or impair bringing additional voices to the shared governance table. For instance, Hutchens and Fernandez (2018) have raised the issue of flipping the tenure debate in higher education. They contend that too often there exists a tendency to frame faculty speech and academic freedom rights as somehow needing to be circumscribed because such rights are not extended to those in administrative positions. The authors argue for another perspective, suggesting that such conversations should be re-framed to ask, instead, *why not* extend professional speech protections, like those possessed by tenure-stream faculty, to other professional staff on campus, including those in student affairs. The concept of shared governance is dependent upon the ability of individuals to participate in governance-related conversations and debates without the fear of retaliation. As such, Hutchens and Fernandez argue for a reinvigoration of faculty speech rights alongside an expansion of professional speech protections to other members of the campus community.

As covered in Chapter One, higher education has been characterized in recent decades by a movement toward corporatization and neo-liberal methods of operation that emphasize the managerial prerogatives in institutional functioning, often at the expense of authentic shared governance. The *Garcetti* case, covered in the previous section, raises the question of to what extent and how should institutions provide spaces for employees to provide open and direct feedback as part of including their voices in institutional decision-making and shared governance.

Recognizing the importance of unfettered participation in shared governance matters, some institutions adopted provisions post *Garcetti* that clarify the importance participation in shared governance matters (Jaschik, 2013; Jaschik, 2009). For instance, the University of California has adopted a policy that refutes the *Garcetti* standards when it comes to faculty speech rights on campus (Jaschik, 2013). The addition to the institution's Statement on the Professional Rights of Faculty provides that faculty have the "freedom to address any matter of institutional policy or action when acting as a member of the faculty whether or not as a member of an agency of institutional governance" (Jaschik, 2013).

Many institutions are at an important tipping point in shared governance and the participation of members of campus community. As originally envisioned from the employee side of participation, shared governance was focused on members of the faculty and the importance of tenure in helping to protect faculty voice and participation in shared governance. Key shifts in higher education, however, mean that a predominant focus on faculty in shared governance leaves out other key campus employee constituencies. For instance, the percentage of faculty members in tenure-stream positions has steadily declined in recent decades (AAUP, n.d.). This means that much of the teaching and faculty service in colleges and universities now resides with non-tenure-track faculty, including those with part-time appointments. A number of non-faculty professionals on campus, including many working in student affairs positions, also carry out roles and duties critical for student success and well-being.

From a flipped perspective, the question arises of why limit free speech protections, including those related to shared governance, to an ever-shrinking number of faculty in tenure-stream positions? Instead, institutions should consider ways to broaden avenues of free speech and expression on campus, including on shared governance matters. Such an approach is counter to the trends that have occurred at many institutions. Reversing such trends will not be easy. Rather than rhetoric, institutions will have to consider how to put policies and procedures in place that elevate the importance of multiple voices in shared governance matters, including those of student affairs professional.

CONCLUSION

In the summer of 2020, we witnessed the power of people across the United States and the globe to advocate for racial justice in social institutions, including an end to police violence against Black people. During this time, calls also came for colleges and universities to reform and to address ongoing racism, to go further than issue the usual statements of support and abstract pledges to do better. To do so, colleges and universities will have to make meaningful commitments to change the ways in which they operate and how decisions are made, including in the realm of shared governance. The erosion of tenure, court decisions that limit the speech rights of public employees, and increasing reliance on managerial authority in running institutions present serious challenges to the meaningful reinvigoration and expansion of shared governance in higher education. Reversing these trends will not be simple and must go beyond rhetoric. However, reinvigorating mechanisms of shared governance and empowering the voices of student affairs professionals–along with students and faculty off the tenure stream–are important ways to help re-make our institutions to operate in ways that are more equitable and socially just.

REFLECTION QUESTIONS

1. Do you supervise student employees (or have you at any point in your career)? What, if anything, did you share with them about speech and their role as student staff? Do you see any distinction when it comes to student employee speech for students who are serving in more clerical or technical roles (like desk clerks or information technology aides) and those serving in paraprofessional roles (such as resident assistants or peer career advisors)?
2. What steps do you take, if any, to distinguish your private speech from your speech as an employee?
3. What is your response to the suggestion of flipping the discussion on tenure protection as discussed in this chapter?

Chapter 7

POLICY, POLICY PROCESS, AND SHARED GOVERNANCE

What is policy? Fowler (2013), while acknowledging a range of definitions, defines policy as "the dynamic and value-laden process through which a political system handles a public problem. It includes government's expressed intentions and official enactments, as well as its consistent patterns of activity and inactivity" (p. 5). The author states that when trying "to determine what the policy really is," that "statute law" is one of the initial sources to consult (Fowler, 2013, p. 6). As Fowler notes, individuals using the term law often are referring to statutes, which are laws passed by state legislatures or the U.S. Congress. Similarly, as Kaplin, Lee, Hutchens, and Rooksby (2019) explain, internal and external sources of law exist for colleges and universities. Internal law refers to "rules and regulations promulgated by individual institutions" (Kaplin et al., 2019, p. 41). External sources of law described by the authors are important for the overview of policy—and are discussed more in Chapter Five—and include federal and state constitutions, statutes passed by individual states and the federal government, and administrative rules and regulations.

STATUTES, RULEMAKING, AND POLICY STAKEHOLDERS

A statute can be viewed as representing an express declaration of public policy intent. Alongside the federal government and state governments, local statutes can be passed by governmental bodies that include cities and counties (Kaplin et al., 2019). As covered in Chapter Five, states have enacted specific laws affecting higher education in such areas as legislation related to postsecondary governance or oversight, such as defining the powers of a state higher education governing or coordinating board. State statutes also often set terms for licensure requirements for professions, such as for teachers, physicians, or counselors. The federal government, which has become increasingly active in higher education since the 1960s, has statutes focused on higher education, with the Higher Education Act perhaps the most notable. The federal government also has put important laws in place, including laws of general application but that encompass colleges and universities, such as legal provisions that prohibit discrimination against students or employees on the basis of such factors as race, sex, or disability (Kaplin et al., 2019). In short, an array of statutory law at the state and federal levels apply to the operations of colleges and universities, with these statutory provisions an important facet of policy and the policy process in terms of higher education.

Fowler (2013), while describing statutory law and policy as interrelated and overlapping, does not interpret them as identical. For instance, statutes are often broadly worded, and regulations and other guidance documents issues by governmental agencies, such as the U.S. Department of Education, serve to give more specific direction on the interpretation and implementation of statutes. Numerous federal regulations provide direction on how colleges and universities can comply with the requirements of federal law, such as the Family Educational Rights and Privacy Act (FERPA), the Higher Education Act (HEA), which, among its provisions deals with federal financial aid support for students, or Title IX, which requires educational institutions receiving federal funds not to discriminate on the basis of sex.

After a statute is enacted, regulations often need to be created by the agency empowered to enforce and interpret the law's provisions to instruct entities covered by the law, such as colleges or universities, on how to adhere to adhere to the law's requirements (Fowler, 2013; Office of the Federal Registrar, n.d.). Federal and state agencies are tasked with implementing and enforcing legal requirements in statutory law. At the top of agency authority are regulations promulgated by agencies "that have the status of law and are as binding as a statute would be" (Kaplin et al., 2019, p. 36). There is also an assortment of less-binding guidance from administrative agencies, such as "dear colleague," letters that are issued by federal agencies. While not receiving the same deference from courts as regulations, such interpretive guidance can be helpful to parties, such as colleges and universities, in understanding how to comply with legal requirements. The enactment of a new law may be the reason for an agency to undertake the rulemaking process. But, as the Office of the Federal Registrar states (n.d.), when engaging in rulemaking, rather than only because of the passage of a new law, agencies often are seeking to respond to issues or events that arise under an existing area of legal authority for the agency, including:

- New technologies or new data on existing issues.
- Concerns arising from accidents or various problems affecting society.
- Recommendations from Congressional committees or federal advisory committees.
- Petitions from interest groups, corporations, and members of the public.
- Lawsuits filed by interest groups, corporations, States, and members of the public.
- Presidential directives.
- "Prompt letters" from the Office of Management and Budget (OMB).
- Requests from other agencies.
- Studies and recommendations of agency staff. ("How does an agency decide to begin rulemaking," para. 2)

In creating or updating regulations, federal agencies must follow the "rule making" process and adhere to the standards contained in the Administrative Procedure Act (Kaplin et al., 2019, p. 37; Office of the Federal Registrar, n.d.). Additionally, what is known as negotiated rule making is often an important part of the process followed by federal agencies to issue formal rules for statutes under their authority (Lubbers, 2018). In this process, which was created by Congress in the Negotiated Rulemaking Act and is an alternative to the traditional rulemaking process, an agency looks to take into account the views of various stakeholders in an effort to reach consensus for a proposed rule. Usually, for the negotiated rule making process, a committee is formed that is intended to be representative of various stakeholders. Meetings are usually open to the public and public comments are often part of the process. The goal is for the committee to reach consensus on language for the proposed rule. Such consensus can occur, but it often does not. When there is not consensus, the federal agency, while including points of consensus in the final rule, is able to draft the language for the rule. In contrast to the negotiated rulemaking process, under the traditional method of rulemaking, the agency issues a proposed rule and then receives comments and feedback. The negotiated rulemaking process endeavors to reduce adversary that can exist in the traditional or standard rulemaking process, though the negotiated rulemaking process can also produce sharp disagreements among stakeholders. While it has only been used once thus far, an agency regulation can be invalidated by Congress and the president or by Congress only if it overrides a presidential veto (Office of the Federal Registrar, n.d.). Whether using the traditional or negotiated rulemaking process, a validly enacted rule issued by a federal agency is considered to have the force of law.

Within the overall regulatory and rulemaking process, including when a negotiated rulemaking process is followed, there are multiple stakeholders and actors that participate and seek to influence regulations, the regulatory process, and the agencies charged with interpreting and enforcing various laws (Kaplin et al., 2019). In the context of higher education and student affairs, an acronym-laden list of professional organizations is active in seeking to influence regulations and policy, with the following just a sampling: NASPA: Student Affairs Administrators in Higher Education, ACPA: College Student Educators International, the Association for Student Conduct Administration (ASCA), the American Council on Education (ACE), the American Association of Community Colleges (AACC), the American Association of University Professors (AAUP), the Association of Public and Land Grant Universities (APLU), and the National Association of Independent Colleges and Universities (NAICU).

Some organizations consist of institutional members, like the American Council on education, and others, alongside institutional membership, also provide individual membership, such as NASPA, or may consist of individual members. Alongside supporting institutions and individuals in serving students, in providing professional development opportunities, and in supporting research, these organizations often seek to influence policy and the regulatory process. Organizational leaders may seek to play an active role in the policy process, such as through regular meetings with congressional leaders and their staff, with staff of the presidential administration, and with other executive branch staff at administrative agencies such as the U.S. Department of Education. These professional organizations also often employ one or more staff in policy positions to monitor regulatory and policy developments, to provide updates to membership, and, drawing upon member feedback and expertise, to advocate for (or against) provisions in proposed regulations or changes to existing law or regulations. Additionally, individuals and institutions often have employees with responsibility for state and federal relations, which can include efforts to influence the policy process.

There also exist advocacy or special interest organizations that that seek to influence statutes and regulations affecting higher education, either as primary focus of their organizational emphasis or as a part of their overall mission. A small listing of such organizations includes the Foundation for Individual Rights in Education (FIRE), the Student Press Law Center (SPLC), the American Civil Liberties Union (ACLU), UnidosUS, and the Christian Legal Society (CLS). There are numerous other examples of advocacy organizations seeking to influence policy issues that impact higher education. Just as with professional organizations, these groups can play important roles in influencing policy and regulations.

Alongside a push to influence federal policy, organizations may also be active in advocating for particular statutes and policies at the state level. One example of an organization that has been particularly active and effective is the American Legislative Exchange Council (ALEC). ALEC, considered a conservative-leaning organization, has been influential in introducing "model legislation" on a wide array of issues in a number of states in an effort to influence the policy and regulatory process, including legislation that can impact colleges and universities (e.g., Bauer-Wolf, 2019; Winn, Sergent, & Madhani, 2019).

For a higher education-specific example of model legislation, the Goldwater Institute has been active in promoting campus speech legislation (Kurtz, Manley, & Butcher, n.d.). As states legislatures have considered the enactment of campus speech laws, the Goldwater Institute's model legislation has provided one template for legislatures to consider. Other organizations, such as FIRE, have also weighed in with campus speech legislative proposals. Campus speech legislation illustrates how organizations can seek to influence statutory law and agency rules and policies, at both the federal and state levels. Efforts to influence law and policy can come from a number of sources, including, as noted, higher education institutions or systems, professional organizations, and interest and advocacy groups. Some interest groups or organizations are specific to higher education, such as the AAUP. Others may have a more general portfolio of interests, such as the ACLU, but can focus periodically on issues specific to or impacting colleges and universities.

This section focused on providing an overview of the what of statutes and policy and the who in terms of illustrative policy players with interest in higher education. The next section turns to the policy process and the *how* of policymaking and interpretation.

THE POLICY PROCESS

Multiple theories exist to account for the policy process. Fowler (2013) describes the policy process as "the sequence of events that occurs when a political system considers different approaches to public problems, adopts one of them, tries it out, and evaluates it" (p. 14). Weible and Sabatier's edited volume *Theories of the Policy Process* (2018) provides a helpful overview of some of the most notable theories and frameworks that explain the policy process. While an extensive review of all policy frameworks is beyond the scope of this work, higher education and student affairs professionals can benefit from an understanding of how application of one or more frames or theories related to the policy process can enhance their sensemaking of how policy is formed at the national and state levels. Such theories and frameworks can also be helpful in understanding how internal institutional policy is crafted and how state and federal policy imperatives are implemented at the campus level.

In classifying policy theories and frameworks, Sabatier (2007), writing in an earlier edition of *Theories of the Policy Process,* provided a still useful explanation for how, until the 1980s, that most such frameworks sought to separate the "policy process into a series of stages—usually agenda setting, policy formation and legitimation, implementation, and evaluation. . ." (Sabatier, 2007, p. 6). New theories and framework would emerge that sought to explain the policymaking process. For example, Institutional Rational Choice provides a "family of frameworks focusing on how institutional rules alter the behavior of intendedly rational individuals motivated by material self-interest" (Sabatier, 2007, p. 8). Or, the Punctuated-Equilibrium Framework posits that "policymaking in the United States is characterized by long periods of incremental change punctuated by brief periods of major policy change" (Sabatier, 2007, p. 9). Scholars have also created critical frameworks to apply to engaging in policy analysis in educational contexts–see, for example, Young & Diem (2018). Given the professional imperative of student affairs professionals to address issues of injustice and discrimination, critical policy lenses can be especially important and informative in helping to frame and address policy issues affecting students and institutions.

A framework, one that helps to explain policymaking at state and federal levels and that can also be helpful at the institutional level, is the Advocacy Coalition Framework, which "focuses on the intersection of advocacy coalitions–each consisting of actors from a variety of institutions who share a set of policy beliefs–within a policy subsystem" (Sabatier, 2007, p. 9). Similarly, the Policy Diffusion Framework looks at how a policy innovation can be adopted across states, a phenomenon that has important implications for higher education. This framework also aligns with and complements understandings of how colleges and universities look to institutional peers and aspirational peers in shaping their organizational identities (Miller, 2019).

Kingdon (2011) proposed influential ideas on how particular topics or issues come to be part of a *policy agenda* and the subsequent steps in the policy-making process. Specifically, he divided the process into the following: (1) agenda setting; (2) identifying policy "alternatives" to address an issue that has made it onto the agenda, (3) a decision point among alternatives, such as the passage of a statute, and (4) and implementation of a policy choice (Kingdon, pp. 2–3). Within these domains, Kingdon (2011) defines the policy agenda as "the list of subjects or problems to which governmental officials, and people outside of governmental closely affiliated with those officials, are paying some serious attention at any given time" (p. 3). He discusses how given the array of issues that can demand the time and attention of governmental officials, "they do in fact seriously attend to some rather than others" (p. 3). For instance, an item may become a prominent agenda item, but such interest may not result in the passage of legislation or action by the president.

Items may also be subject to a change in status under these domains, representing how policy issues are often contested. For example, the legal status of undocumented individuals who came to the United States as young children has garnered considerable attention and advocacy from interest organizations, and former President Barrack Obama issued an executive order to provide a legal status for these individuals–the Deferred Action for Childhood Arrivals (DACA) (Hesson, 2020). But Congress failed and has continued to fail to enact to provide a process through statute for these individuals to have legal residency status and a path to citizenship, despite multiple attempts. And following the election of President Donald Trump, he ordered an end to the program enacted during the Obama administration. Lower federal courts blocked Trump's actions, and the U.S. Supreme Court has agreed to review the legality of Trump's action. The twists and turns of the DACA program show how policy issues are often contested and subject to change depending on shifting political winds. Rather than static, policy issues are often subject to political disputes and can evolve over time.

Kingdon (2011) also discusses how multiple agendas can exist. Different governmental actors and their advisors may have specific, specialized agendas. In relation to items that are on the agenda of particular policy decisionmakers, Kingdon talks about the particular *alternatives* that are being considered by policy actors to address an item on the agenda. Another important aspect that Kingdon covers relates to the range of actors seeking to influence the governmental agenda and the alternatives to be adopted in addressing an issue or problem. As he covers, a governmental agenda may change depending on the outcome of elections, such as what happened to the issue of providing legal residency and citizenship to undocumented individuals after the election of Donald Trump. Or an event can push an item onto the policy agenda, with the recent COVID-19 pandemic a startling reminder of how an event can quickly move to the top of the policy agenda. As to policy participants within government, the federal government specifically, there are Congress, congressional staff members, the president (including presidential staff and political appointees), and civil service employees in administrative agencies. Kingdon (2011) suggests that civil service employees, such as at federal agencies like the U.S. Department of Education, may play a lesser role in agenda setting but may by exert more influence over implementation and policy alternatives. While policy process models can sometimes make policy adoption and implication appear as a rational and orderly state of affairs, the actual policy process can be much more disjointed and unclear (Kingdon, 2011).

There are also non-governmental actors that can influence the policy agenda and the alternatives under consideration. Such individual and organizational actors can come from advocacy groups or professional or industry organizations, such as ones mentioned earlier in the chapter. Along with seeking to have items placed on the policy agenda and alternatives, interest groups may seek to block an item from being placed on the policy agenda or considered as an alternative for adoption (Kingdon, 2011). Kingdon also discusses how ideas from academics, researchers, and consultants can make their way into the policy process, such as by being picked up by congressional staffers or being advocated by an interest group. The media can also bring attention to particular issues, thus helping an item to gain traction. Movements can also have grassroots origins. For instance, while Kingdon wrote about traditional media sources, social media also represents a way that ideas can be communicated and shared and promote activity and activism. Protests and calls across the United States and the world for reform to address racism and police violence against Black individuals and general systemic racism in summer 2020 showed the power of collective action and the potential to affect law, policy, and practice, including proposed police reform legislation introduced by Democratic leadership in Congress (Nilson & Zhou, 2020).

While policy change can happen quickly, especially in response to pivotal events, such as a pandemic, this is not always the case. One important takeaway about the policy process is that some policies can develop and evolve in an incremental way. At times, an incremental approach can be looked down upon as not being decisive or bold, but, over time, incremental changes can result in helpful changes. An incremental approach, one guided by a clear vision, may make it possible to achieve meaningful improvement over time. Such a process may also make it easier to get "buy in" from various actors than a policy that affects multiple systems and seeks to promote significant change at one time. At the same time, incremental approaches may hinder needed change and blunt efforts to aid students and employees.

THE GARBAGE CAN MODEL AND POLICY FORMATION

Another helpful contribution from Kingdon (2011) is consideration of the garbage can model to policy agenda setting and alternatives. Looking to Cohen, March, and Olsen (1972), Kingdon discusses how "problems, solutions, participants, and choice opportunities" each "has a life of its own, largely unrelated to the others" (p. 85). He describes a system in which a potential choice opportunity

> floats by in the organization (e.g., a university), various participants, each with their own resources become involved. Various problems (e.g., maintaining scholarly quality, curriculum improvement, affirmative action) are introduced into the choice, and various solutions (e.g., inside candidates for a deanship, outside candidates, expanding the unit, abolishing the unit) may be considered. (Kingdon, 2011, p. 85)

Continuing, Kingdon (2011) states that a choice opportunity can be viewed as a garbage can into which problems and solutions are placed as they are generated. In this garbage can, a solution can be viewed as needing to be attached to a problem.

Separating a potential problem from a solution can be helpful for those advocating for policy changes at any level, including on campus. An individual or group may view a policy alternative as addressing an issue of importance. For example, at the campus level, a group of student activists may view campus recycling and other environmental measures as vital in light of growing environmental and climate challenges from global warming. While inherently important, such motivations may not move campus leaders to take action and enhance campus recycling efforts. However, institutions face ongoing financial challenges and are constantly looking for ways to conserve financial resources. A recycling plan that can, for instance, save an institution on the cost of transporting waste to an off-site landfill may align with institutional cost-saving initiatives. Thus, the environmental problem sought to be addressed by the campus advocates is not necessarily the same problem of actionable interest from institutional leaders. However, the student activists can attach their "solution" to a "problem"—that of limited financial resources—that is on the ongoing policy agenda of campus leaders. Policy entrepreneurs, as Kingdon (2011) identifies them, can further their own agendas by realizing that a solution or alternative that is important to them can be cast in multiple ways, which may help an issue gain greater traction in the policy process.

At the same time, it can be important to advocate for a policy choice on its particular merits, including social justice grounds, and reorienting a policy problem or issue on pragmatic grounds can raise concerns. For instance, in addressing issues confronting populations who are marginalized and discriminated against on our campuses based on such reasons as race, gender identity, sexual orientation, or disability, their civil rights and rights to equitable treatment deserve attention because of the inherent value of all individuals.

Legal debates over affirmative action reveal some of the concerns of grounding policy solutions on pragmatic legal grounds. In *Grutter v. Bollinger* (2003) and in a subsequent case, *Fisher v. University Texas at Austin* (2016), the U.S. Supreme Court approved of the use of race as one factor in higher education admissions as a means to help colleges and universities achieve the educational benefits of diversity to all students in assembling a more diverse student body. While *Grutter* and *Fisher* stand as important legal victories in efforts to defend the legal use of affirmative action in higher education, the Supreme Court's reasoning was not predominantly grounded in addressing ongoing general societal and institutional discrimination against students based on race. The rationale used by the Supreme Court to uphold race-conscious admissions—the overall educational benefits of a diverse student population—has been critiqued as a justification that shifts a focus on race-conscious admissions away from past and ongoing discrimination based on race (see, e.g., Goldstein Hode & Meisenbach, 2016). Legal battles over affirmative action in higher education admissions are a powerful prompt of how taking a pragmatic approach to policy entrepreneurship—while often a useful tactic—should not displace, even unintentionally, equity and social justice concerns that are at the core of many policy goals and policy problems in higher education.

Kingdon (2011) describes how the various streams of problems, politics, and policy can join together, creating a *policy window* in which to gain approval for a policy enactment. A policy window can be a time for an individual or a group with a solution in hand to attach it to a problem that has made it on to the governmental policy agenda. Or a potential policy may flow in a more linear fashion as a problem is placed on the policy agenda. Policy windows may become open because of changes in political administration. In higher education, at the campus level, a change in institutional or system leadership may serve to open a policy window. Or pressing events, such as an enrollment drop, may help to open a policy window for policy entrepreneurs to be able to act and to advance their policy ideas. Other events, such as ones gaining widespread public attention or advocacy by interest groups, can also open policy windows. Recent movements for institutions, including colleges and universities, to address systemic racism and racial injustice show the power of collective action to bring about policy change.

POLICY IMPLEMENTATION AND STREET-LEVEL BUREAUCRATS

After a policy is adopted, an important phase is entered into–that of implementation. Implementation is often the point in the larger policy process where colleges and universities will have to put internal institutional standards and policies in place to carry out a policy from the state or the federal government, such as regulations from the U.S. Department of Education. The manner in which a policy is implemented by on-the-ground actors is very important in terms of achieving the goals of an overarching policy. Implementation is dependent upon factors that include a willingness among stakeholders charged with carrying out policy directives to show fidelity to the policy and the availability of resources to carry out a policy. There can also be important unintended consequences that can occur when a policy is implemented.

The Prohibition movement–which resulted in making the sale and distribution of most alcohol illegal in the United State from 1920 to 1933–provides a historic example of the failures of a policy achieving its intended results, not having the resources for implementation, and the impact of unintended consequences. The prohibition of alcohol, which was buttressed by nativist, racially discriminatory, and classist beliefs among many adherents, was viewed by supporters as a way to ameliorate all kinds of social ills in American life (Okrent, 2010). The belief in some quarters in the transformational power of prohibition helped lead, at least in part, to the adoption of at least two constitutional amendments. The Sixteenth Amendment authorized the federal government to collect income taxes and was motivated, at least in some measures by many supporters of prohibition, as a way to help replace federal revenue that would come from the loss of federal taxes on alcohol. And, in 1919, the Eighteenth Amendment was ratified, which banned the production, transportation, and sale of most alcohol in the United States.

Rather than ameliorating all forms of social ills, as envisioned by supporters, the enactment of prohibition failed on a monumental scale (Okrent, 2010). There existed little support for prohibition among many individuals, and the law was often violated outright or circumvented through exceptions in the law, the Volstead Act, passed to carry out the goals of the Eighteenth Amendment, such as those for sacramental or medicinal purposes. Making most alcohol use illegal also helped inadvertently to lay the groundwork for the rise of organized crime in the United States. In terms of implementation, the federal government also provided very little funding for enforcement of prohibition. The unmitigated disaster of the amendment, which resulted in an implementation that failed on multiple levels and triggered unintended consequences, helped lead to the passage of another constitutional amendment, the Twenty-first Amendment, to repeal prohibition.

Rather than an afterthought to policy formation, implementation represents a vital step in the policy process. An otherwise well-crafted policy can fail to achieve desired goals if appropriate attention and resources are not directed toward implementation. As Brower, Jones, Tandberg, Hu, and Park (2017) note, the term "street-level-bureaucrat" has been used to describe those public employees "who interact directly with citizens in the course of their jobs, and who have substantial discretion in the execution of their work" (p. 809; quoting from Lipsky, 1980, p. 3). The term also fits for many campus employees at both public and private institutions who work directly with students and are often at the point of service in actually implementing a policy, whether one with an internal campus impetus or one prompted by external action. Thus, just as stakeholder feedback is an important part of policy design, implementation benefits from an inclusive approach. In relation to student affairs, an inclusive approach means taking into account the voices and feedback of staff who are directly charged with carrying out a policy—campus street-level bureaucrats—and also incorporating the views of others integral to implementation, including students and faculty. Importantly, an inclusive approach to policy formation and implementation also aligns with principles of shared governance.

A study of developmental education reform in Florida by Brower et al. (2017) shows how the views of front-line implementers are integral into how a policy is actually carried out. The authors examined how the 28 colleges comprising the Florida College System (FCS) responded to a state law that exempted active-duty military personnel and individuals who attended high school in Florida since ninth grade and had graduated with a standard Florida high school diploma from having to enroll in developmental education courses. The law meant that, for covered students, public colleges could not require placement tests that could be used to enroll certain students in non-credit earning developmental education. The law also had an advising component applicable to all students. In response to the law, implementation teams were created at the various FCS campuses. These teams had to deal with issues that included sorting out students who were and were not exempt from developmental education courses.

The researchers, focused on the implementation approached as the various campuses, created a typology to describe how campus personnel (i.e., street-level-bureaucrats) responded to the law and the resulting interactions with implementation. One campus response was *oppositional implementation* in which campus street-level-bureaucrats "actively resist[ed] a policy directive through actions that defy the provisions of the policy" (Brower et al., 2017, p. 819). Individuals at this campus largely viewed the legislation as potentially harmful to student success. As such, they sought support from the employee union to challenge the policy, and, once the law was passed, encouraged students who were exempt to enroll in developmental education courses.

Another institutional response that came from the study was *circumventing implementation,* which the authors described as "resisting a policy directive through intentional inaction or actions that sidestep or circumvent the provisions of the policy" (Brower et al., 2017, p. 821). Behaviors associated with this response included slowness in launching the policy and "selective implementation," which consisted of letting students know that they were exempt from developmental education courses only if the student inquired about their status in relation to developmental education courses.

A third approach response to the law found among campuses in the system was a *satisficing implementation* approach (Brower et al.,

2017, p. 823), which encompassed "passively cooperating with a policy directive through actions that are minimally compliant with the requirements of the policy" (p. 823). At one campus, the researchers found that faculty resisted making changes to their gateway courses that now would be enrolling students who were exempt from having to take developmental education courses. The researchers characterized this approach as playing dumb, in which campus actors "adopt[ed] a literal interpretation of the statute regardless of negative consequences," which consisted of a larger numbers of students failing gateway courses than previously rather than adjusting the courses to account for the enrollment of students who were now exempt from first taking developmental education courses. Another response at this campus was to "service rationing" to "curtail the time spent on each student during new student orientation and advising sessions" (p. 824). Under this approach, the campus nominally implemented the policy but made no real changes in how it was delivering and teaching courses and providing additional services.

A final approach identified by the researchers was that of *facilitative implementation,* which involves "actively complying with a policy directive through actions that exert maximum effort to find novel solutions to problems presented by the policy" (Brower et al., 2017, p. 825). Under this approach, one campus adopted strategies that included the reallocation of people and other resources and improvising in an effort to show fidelity to the policy goals. Street-level-bureaucrats at this campus embraced the policy and were willing to change and be flexible in how they interpreted and sought to implement the law.

In taking stock of these responses to the policy, the researchers discussed how "opposition to the legislation was the most common perspective among street-level bureaucrats," with campus actors expressing concern over the negative impact the policy would have on students (Brower et al., 2017, p. 826). The study serves as a useful higher education example of how policies in higher education "do not implement themselves; they require campus personnel knowledge to ensure that mandates meet the objectives established by legislators. The knowledge of street-level bureaucrats can be used to work for or against successful implementation" (Brower et al., 2017, 828-29; citing Lipsky, 1980). The authors suggest that street-level bureaucrats are more likely to "oppose legislation when they feel powerless in the legislative process, lack inclusion and discretion over implementation plans within their organization, and question whether the legislation is good for society and their clients" (Brower et al., 2017, p. 829). The researchers note the need for legislation to contain sound "policy rationales," the importance of seeking public comment, "especially among street-level bureaucrats," and providing sufficient autonomy to street-level bureaucrats in how a policy is implemented (p. 829). The study provides an instructive example of the importance of implementation in the policy process and the benefits of an inclusive approach to policy formation and implementation.

CONCLUSION

Rather than following a simple, linear path, policy formation and implementation are often characterized by complexity, nuance, and starts and stops in the process. A policy "solution" can proceed the identification of a policy "problem" by policymakers. There are multiple organizations and actors that can influence the policy process at various stages. While some actors may seek to advance a proposed policy, others may be acting in opposition. An otherwise sound policy can be thwarted by failures in implementation. Given the complexities and obstacles that can arise in policy formation and implementation, familiarity with concepts and theories about the policy process and policy actors and stakeholders can help empower student affairs professionals to become more effective policy entrepreneurs. Lessons from the policy literature also reinforce the value of shared governance. More equitable and effective policies arise from the participation of multiple stakeholders in the campus policy process. A campus policy formulated with insufficient input from an array of stakeholders, including the campus street-level bureaucrats charged with implementing the policy, may face hurdles in implementation and may fail to adhere to institutional values, including those related to social justice and inclusion. Conversely, an inclusive approach to campus policy and implementation is more likely to result in policies that are in alignment with an institution's mission and less likely to face hurdles in implementation.

REFLECTION QUESTIONS

1. What are the top three to five state-level or national policy issues which are having a significant impact on your work or student experience on campus? What are the arenas in which those policies are being addressed? How do those policy issues play out in shared governance deliberations?
2. What are the top two to three institutional-level policy issues which are having a significant impact on your work or student experience on campus? What are the shared governance structures in which those policies are being addressed?
3. Who are the street-level bureaucrats (Brower, Jones, Tandberg, Hu, & Park, 2017) on your campus who are shaping institutional enactment on the policy decisions for the items you mentioned above? Which of the four identified tactics do you see being used by those employees?
4. What do you see as the relationship between healthy shared governance on a campus and effective development and enactment of institution-level policies?

Chapter 8

THEMES, THOUGHTS, AND THINGS TO DO

> *Governance is fundamental to the way in which decisions are made in universities. Governance allows us to answer questions such as: In which forum should a decision be made? Who are legitimate members of the forum? What are the terms under which the decision is legitimate? . . . But, although it provides answers to these questions, governance is still not an end to itself. Rather, it is a process towards the end or towards the achievement of desired outcomes, and the end is legitimated through the process. Hence, legitimization through the correct process is the sine qua non of collegial governance, policy formulation, and decision-making in the academy.*
>
> Austin and Jones (2016, pp. 149–150))

Throughout the preceding chapters we have explored shared governance in American higher education with a particular focus on the ways in which student affairs professionals can help foster and strengthen it at their institutions. In this concluding chapter, themes from that exploration will be identified, closing thoughts on shared governance put forward, and a draft of an action plan shared.

THEMES

A number of themes recur throughout this book. Those themes are highlighted here for purposes of clarity and reflection.

Drawing on Helpful Resources to Shape Practice

The first theme is that we can draw on the history, theory, and literature of shared governance, student affairs, and higher education to inform our efforts with regard to shared governance even though there are some noticeable and lamentable gaps in the literature.

Being Open in Our Approach

Another theme is that American higher education is an open and complex system and, therefore, variations exist across higher education in shared governance stakeholders and structures. We ought be as open in our approach to shared governance as higher education is open as a field. Consider the broad context in which a challenge or opportunity is being considered. Think clearly and deeply about what is merely the presenting question and what is the actual question at hand. Identify all those who might have a role to play or who might be persuaded to play a role.

Recognizing and Addressing Privilege and Oppression

Just as higher education is an open system, it is also a system in which privilege and oppression play themselves out in both overt and subtle (though no less powerful) ways. Shared governance is an integral part of that system, and it comes as no surprise then that privilege and oppression are part of the politics, power, and persuasion through which shared governance is enacted on our campuses. They are played out in foundational constructs and in contemporary practices. Recognizing and naming them whenever we see them (in whatever forms they take) in shared governance offers a powerful opportunity to help assure a truly inclusive approach.

Acting Ethically

Another theme throughout the book is the importance of engaging ethically. Three particular dimensions of ethical practice have been stressed repeatedly. They are respecting autonomy, being truthful, and being loyal (including respecting confidences and honoring your role at the institution). When it comes to student affairs professionals and our role in an institution, it starts and ends with the students. Our work in support of their success leads us to our interactions with a host of others both within and outside the institution, and we are well advised to conduct ourselves ethically in all of those dealings.

One might wonder why benefiting others has not been mentioned here. It is certainly not to suggest that one should be indifferent to helping or serving others in the course of doing our work. Rather, it is a recognition that shared governance is an inherently political process in which players act on perceived self-interest. One may well make political choices which seem most likely to lead to the maximally possible desirable outcome, and those choices could require giving up a bit of what the player wants in order to help increase the likelihood of a good outcome.

Earning and Maintaining Trust

The importance of trust in fostering and sustaining good shared governance at an institution is difficult to overstate. One may earn trust through acting ethically in the ways discussed earlier. It can also come as a result of developing a reputation for being accessible and open to discussion. Another way to help build trust is to be sure to keep one's word, being honest about any limitations or points of departure and assuring that promises made are promises kept.

Having Patience

Shared governance is not about efficiency or expediency. It takes time to carefully and thoroughly lay a foundation with shared understandings about purposes, participants, and processes. Then it takes time to work issues through the various structures in a way that honors institutional culture and fully engages all the stakeholders. It often then takes time to figure out exactly how whatever has been decided will be enacted and then to address all the various unintended consequences stemming from the deliberations, decision, and implementation. Attempts to cut corners or step up the pace seem to lead to reduced confidence, increased tensions, and diminished cohesion. There is no substitute for patience in shared governance.

Engaging with Purpose and Intentionality

Making a meaningful contribution to shared governance at your institution is unlikely to come about as the result of some happenstance or coincidence. It is far more likely to begin with a thoughtfully developed sense of purpose for shared governance and your role in it. Hand in hand with a sense of purpose is a spirit of intentionality. Being involved in shared governance seems more likely to achieve the intended purpose if the involvement is intentional, reflecting a thoughtful design of action which is responsive to and tailored for the circumstances at hand.

Demonstrating Commitment

The final theme highlighted here and which appears throughout the book is the value of demonstrating commitment to shared governance. Statements of commitment are not enough; actions must align with expressions. In addition to modeling the behaviors already discussed in this section, commitment, may be evidenced through respect for the recognition and inclusion of democratically elected representatives, adherence to principles of inclusion, utilization of agreed upon structures and processes (rather than looking for opportunities to work around them), and thoughtful acceptance and consideration of advice and decisions born of those structures and processes.

THOUGHTS

As this book moves toward its conclusion, the time has come to share our own perspective on shared governance. Readers may have deduced by now that our own thinking on the subject is similar to that of Birnbaum who writes, "The purpose of academic institutions is not to create products but to embody ideas. Academic governance cannot be rationalized for the same reason that it is not possible to rationalize the purposes for which academic institutions exist" (2004, p. 18). He goes on to share, ". . . the governance of an academic institution is organic, not mechanical. It is not designed so much as it evolves because it uniquely supports the activities of a social institution whose processes and goals cannot be clearly defined, whose outcomes cannot be precisely measured, but whose critical importance to society is indisputable" (Birnbaum, 2004, pp. 18–19).

We are inclined to the notion that it is difficult, if not impossible, to provide a singular simple description of the purposes of higher education. This makes designing and implementing a rational and logical

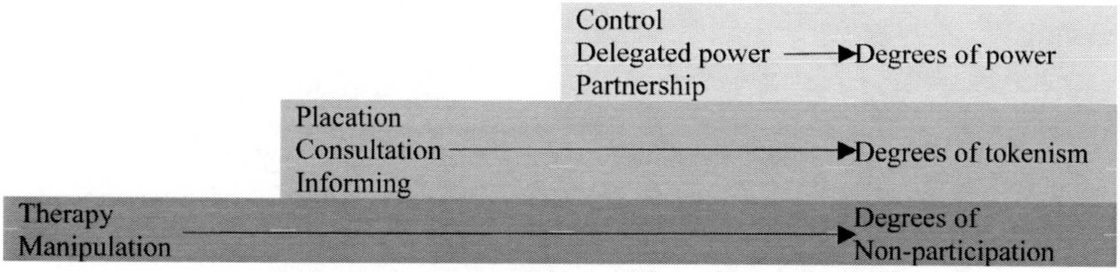

Figure 8.1. Ladder of Progressive Involvement

Source: Adapted from Miller, M. (2003). *Improving faculty governance.* Stillwater, OK: New Forums.

set of shared governance policies and practices an exercise in futility in our opinion. Institutions would be better off recognizing that shared governance is an ideal, or a set of ideals, which mirror back to us and serve as symbol of our highest aspirations for the ways in which educated persons can and should go about building communities in the service of society. Recognizing and embracing the inherent contradictions and tensions associated with such a task, and mindful of the ways in which systemic isms play themselves out in our lives and our obligation to acknowledge and confront those social ills, the stakeholders of higher education at a given institution can, through shared discussion and deliberation, reach agreement on the ways in which the power associated with higher education can be shared for the betterment of all involved. Together they can then wield that power in ways which are socially just, caring, ethical, and impactful to advance human learning and development.

Figure 8.1 shows the progression of involvement of stakeholders in higher education decisionmaking. It is to the highest rung on that ladder to which we should aspire.

THINGS TO DO

Hopefully at this point readers are ready to sign up for what it will take to help fully realize the vision for shared governance on their campuses. The exact steps that could be considered will vary based on the circumstances at a given institution because the particulars of shared governance will deviate based on those details. As Fish (2007,

p. 9) rightfully asserts, "No one should presume to tell a college or university what its governance structure should be. In fact, there's no general model of governance, shared or otherwise, that can be replicated from place to place. Each institution is differently situated with respect to its history and mission; its size; the number and nature of its programs; its relationship to local, state, and national governments; its legal obligations and attendant dangers; its mechanisms of funding' and so on" (Fish, 2007, p. 9).

This is not to say that there is not some general guidance that might be helpful to student affairs professionals (or any other stakeholder partners) who want to get to work in strengthening shared governance. One good place to start is Bejou and Bejou's (2016) list of fifteen principles for shared governance. These items can serve as a solid start to a powerful action plan. The fifteen items are:

1. An elected representative body for the university community as a whole (University Council) and for each component, namely, faculty, staff, and students (Faculty Senate, Staff Senate, SGA)
2. Revision (and periodic evaluation) of the mission/strategic vision of the university to ensure that it is (a) grounded in comprehensive assessment; (b) based on extensive input from all components; (c) reflective of the strategic goals of the board and the president; (d) guided by future educational success; and (e) both understood and supported by faculty, administrators, staff, and students
3. Support (budget, staff, facilities) for the University Council, the Faculty Senate, the Staff Senate, and SGA
4. Full disclosure of—and open and honest access to—all information essential for each committee, council, or senate to effectively and efficiently fulfill its
5. duties and responsibilities
6. Decision-making procedures in which the university president or his or her designee in all practical circumstances receives recommendations on all critical matters of policy and planning from the appropriate governing bodies (such as the University Council, the Faculty Senate, the SGA, or the Staff Senate, and the respective schools) before presenting any action matters for approval to the Board—if the President or his or her designee

disagrees with the recommendations, he or she must provide formal justifications for disapproval to the originating body and should make every possible effort to do so in time for the appropriate governing bodies and the president or his or her designee to possibly reach a compromise position

7. Guaranteed decision-making procedures that allow all constituents a secure seat at the table (i.e., participatory and collaborative decision making that is both transparent and straightforward) and that will in turn enhance mutual respect and trust between different components of the university
8. A truly informative and substantive linkage between the board and the university that guarantees that members of the board are informed about all relevant matters pertaining to the well-being of the university and that must include faculty, staff, and students as members of the board. In addition to the president of the university, the faculty representative shall also serve as the University Council representative on the board.
9. An ever-evolving strategic plan that allows for short-, medium-, and long term planning and evaluation and that is founded on the input of all components of the university, based on their deliberations, expertise, and experience
10. Increased efforts to boost efficiency and responsiveness (this emphatically includes streamlining decision-making processes to meet both internal efficiency standards and externally imposed requirements) and allocate appropriate resources to areas that directly affect the quality of education
11. Increased efforts to identify, hire, and maintain quality personnel as well as advise on the development and implementation of standardized criteria for the evaluation, support, and dismissal of academic or administrative officers
12. Fully developed forms of governance that both allow and encourage academic and administrative officers in leadership positions, as well as all other members of the university community, to be stewards of the entire university, and not just their own constituencies
13. Procedures that ensure that new members of any committee, council, or senate receive orientation or training concerning said organization's operating procedures; mission and goals; as well as past, present, and future agenda

14. Mechanisms that both support and enforce accountability (this means that all constituents need to have sufficient time for deliberation on all important matters that concern the well-being of the university and that all constituents should respond with their input–if at all possible–in generally no more than 30 days)
15. Assurance that all units, programs, support services, initiatives, positions, programs, and so on, both academic and nonacademic, are part of the official university governance system and thus subject to all appropriate oversight and evaluation processes
16. Assurance that the president can establish university committees to assist in the development of policy and in the facilitation of actions required for the orderly administration of the university, so long as said committees do not violate the principles of this University Shared Governance Constitution. (Bejou & Bejou, 2016, pp. 59–60)

CONCLUSION

In closing, we offer three final broad recommendations from the literature on shared governance for consideration by the readers. The first is that we all need to be informed about the consequences of managerialism and neoliberalism in American higher education and the threat that they pose. Here again we turn to Birnbaum. He writes, "There is no crisis of governance among those institutions that emphasize academic as opposed to corporate values. Claims that such institutions are risking disruption or failure because they cannot respond quickly enough to a changing environment are both inaccurate and misplaced" (2004, p. 20). Second, whatever one believes about the purposes and functions of higher education, we are likely to find agreement that those purposes and functions will be better served when all segments of the campus community are fully participating in fulfilling them. Consequently, "the question for college and university governance writ large is how to inform all of its participants–the board, the administration, the students, and the alumni, as well as the faculty–that their participation is critical" (Burgan, 2004, p. xiv). The third and final recommendation flows from the observation that, "when done well, shared governance strengthens the quality of leadership and decision making at an institution, enhances its ability to achieve its vision and meet strategic goals, and increases the odds that the very best thinking by all parties to shared governance is brought to bear on institutional challenges" and "engenders an institutional culture of collective ownership and accountability for the institutions present and future" (Bahls, 2014, p. 3). All of us can act in a spirit of generativity and stewardship through shared governance to maintain the quality of higher education at our colleges and universities. In the words of Hillel the Elder, if not us, who? If not now, when?

REFLECTION QUESTIONS

1. Are there other themes in the book which you feel should be highlighted?
2. What are your thoughts on shared governance and how you might take a greater role in strengthening it on your campus?
3. Using Bejou and Bejou's (2016) 15 necessary items, how well developed to you believe the shared governance infrastructure is for your campus?
4. Who on your campus might be an ally to you in efforts to strengthen shared governance on your campus? Name all that come to mind? How might you approach them about doing this work together?

APPENDIX

AAUP STATEMENT ON GOVERNMENT OF COLLEGES AND UNIVERSITIES

The statement that follows is directed to governing board members, administrators, faculty members, students, and other persons in the belief that the colleges and universities of the United States have reached a stage calling for appropriately shared responsibility and cooperative action among the components of the academic institution. The statement is intended to foster constructive joint thought and action, both within the institutional structure and in protection of its integrity against improper intrusions.

It is not intended that the statement serve as a blueprint for governance on a specific campus or as a manual for the regulation of controversy among the components of an academic institution, although it is to be hoped that the principles asserted will lead to the correction of existing weaknesses and assist in the establishment of sound structures and procedures. The statement does not attempt to cover relations with those outside agencies that increasingly are controlling the resources and influencing the patterns of education in our institutions of higher learning: for example, the United States government, state legislatures, state commissions, interstate associations or compacts, and other interinstitutional arrangements. However, it is hoped that the statement will be helpful to these agencies in their consideration of educational matters.

Students are referred to in this statement as an institutional component coordinate in importance with trustees, administrators, and faculty. There is, however, no main section on students. The omission has two causes: (1) the changes now occurring in the status of American students have plainly outdistanced the analysis by the educational community, and an attempt to define the situation without thorough study might prove unfair to student interests, and (2) students do not in fact at present have a significant voice in the government of colleges and universities; it would be unseemly to obscure, by superficial equality of length of statement, what may be a serious lag entitled to separate and full confrontation.

The concern for student status felt by the organizations issuing this statement is embodied in a note, "On Student Status," intended to stimulate the educational community to turn its attention to an important need.

This statement was jointly formulated by the American Association of University Professors, the American Council on Education (ACE), and the Association of Governing Boards of Universities and Colleges (AGB). In October 1966, the board of directors of the ACE took action by which its council "recognizes the statement as a significant step forward in the clarification of the respective roles of governing boards, faculties, and administrations," and "commends it to the institutions which are members of the Council." The Council of the AAUP adopted the statement in October 1966, and the Fifty-third Annual Meeting endorsed it in April 1967. In November 1966, the executive committee of the AGB took action by which that organization also "recognizes the statement as a significant step forward in the clarification of the respective roles of governing boards, faculties, and administrations," and "commends it to the governing boards which are members of the Association." (In April 1990, the Council of the AAUP adopted several changes in language in order to remove gender-specific references from the original text.)

Source: https://www.aaup.org/report/statement-government-colleges-and-universities

1. Introduction

This statement is a call to mutual understanding regarding the government of colleges and universities. Understanding, based on community of interest and producing joint effort, is essential for at least three reasons. First, the academic institution, public or private, often has become less autonomous; buildings, research, and student tuition are supported by funds over which the college or university exercises a diminishing control. Legislative and executive governmental authorities, at all levels, play a part in the making of important decisions in academic policy. If these voices and forces are to be successfully heard and integrated, the academic institution must be in a position to meet them with its own generally unified view. Second, regard for the welfare of the institution remains important despite the mobility and interchange of scholars. Third, a college or university in which all the components are aware of their interdependence, of the usefulness of communication among themselves, and of the force of joint action will enjoy increased capacity to solve educational problems.

2. The Academic Institution: Joint Effort

a. Preliminary Considerations

The variety and complexity of the tasks performed by institutions of higher education produce an inescapable interdependence among governing board, administration, faculty, students, and others. The relationship calls for adequate communication among these components, and full opportunity for appropriate joint planning and effort.

Joint effort in an academic institution will take a variety of forms appropriate to the kinds of situations encountered. In some instances, an initial exploration or recommendation will be made by the president with consideration by the faculty at a later stage; in other instances, a first and essentially definitive recommendation will be made by the faculty, subject to the endorsement of the president and the governing board. In still others, a substantive contribution can be made when student leaders are responsibly involved in the process. Although the variety of such approaches may be wide, at least two general conclusions regarding joint effort seem clearly warranted: (1) important areas of action involve at one time or another the initiating capacity and decision-making participation of all the institutional components, and (2) differences in the weight of each voice, from one point to the next, should be determined by reference to the responsibility of each component for the particular matter at hand, as developed hereinafter.

b. Determination of General Educational Policy

The general educational policy, i.e., the objectives of an institution and the nature, range, and pace of its efforts, is shaped by the institutional charter or by law, by tradition and historical development, by the present needs of the community of the institution, and by the professional aspirations and standards of those directly involved in its work. Every board will wish to go beyond its formal trustee obligation to conserve the accomplishment of the past and to engage seriously with the future; every faculty will seek to conduct an operation worthy of scholarly standards of learning; every administrative officer will strive to meet his or her charge and to attain the goals of the institution. The interests of all are coordinate and related, and unilateral effort can lead to confusion or conflict. Essential to a solution is a reasonably explicit statement on general educational policy. Operating responsibility and authority, and procedures for continuing review, should be clearly defined in official regulations.

When an educational goal has been established, it becomes the responsibility primarily of the faculty to determine the appropriate curriculum and procedures of student instruction.

Special considerations may require particular accommodations: (1) a publicly supported institution may be regulated by statutory provisions, and (2) a church-controlled institution may be limited by its charter or bylaws. When such external requirements influence course content and the manner of instruction or research, they impair the educational effectiveness of the institution.

Such matters as major changes in the size or composition of the student body and the relative emphasis to be given to the various elements of the educational and research program should involve participation of governing board, administration, and faculty prior to final decision.

c. Internal Operations of the Institution

The framing and execution of long-range plans, one of the most important aspects of institutional responsibility, should be a central and continuing concern in the academic community.

Effective planning demands that the broadest possible exchange of information and opinion should be the rule for communication among the components of a college or university. The channels of communication should be established and maintained by joint endeavor. Distinction should be observed between the institutional system of communication and the system of responsibility for the making of decisions.

A second area calling for joint effort in internal operation is that of decisions regarding existing or prospective physical resources. The board, president, and faculty should all seek agreement on basic decisions regarding buildings and other facilities to be used in the educational work of the institution.

A third area is budgeting. The allocation of resources among competing demands is central in the formal responsibility of the governing board, in the administrative authority of the president, and in the educational function of the faculty. Each component should therefore have a voice in the determination of short- and long-range priorities, and each should receive appropriate analyses of past budgetary experience, reports on current budgets and expenditures, and short- and long-range budgetary projections. The function of each component in budgetary matters should be understood by all; the allocation of authority will determine the flow of information and the scope of participation in decisions.

Joint effort of a most critical kind must be taken when an institution chooses a new president. The selection of a chief administrative officer should follow upon a cooperative search by the governing board and the faculty, taking into consideration the opinions of others who are appropriately interested. The president should be equally qualified to serve both as the executive officer of the governing board and as the chief academic officer of the institution and the faculty. The president's dual role requires an ability to interpret to board and faculty the educational views and concepts of institutional government of the other. The president should have the confidence of the board and the faculty.

The selection of academic deans and other chief academic officers should be the responsibility of the president with the advice of, and in consultation with, the appropriate faculty.

Determinations of faculty status, normally based on the recommendations of the faculty groups involved, are discussed in Part 5 of this statement; but it should here be noted that the building of a strong faculty requires careful joint effort in such actions as staff selection and promotion and the granting of tenure. Joint action should also govern dismissals; the applicable principles and procedures in these matters are well established.[1]

d. External Relations of the Institution

Anyone–a member of the governing board, the president or other member of the administration, a member of the faculty, or a member of the student body or the alumni–affects the institution when speaking of it in public. An individual who speaks unofficially should so indicate. An individual who speaks officially for the institution, the board, the administration, the faculty, or the student body should be guided by established policy.

It should be noted that only the board speaks legally for the whole institution, although it may delegate responsibility to an agent. The right of a board member, an administrative officer, a faculty member, or a student to speak on general educational questions or about the administration and operations of the individual's own institution is a part of that person's right as a citizen and should not be abridged by the institution.[2] There exist, of course, legal bounds relating to defamation of character, and there are questions of propriety.

3. The Academic Institution: The Governing Board

The governing board has a special obligation to ensure that the history of the college or university shall serve as a prelude and inspiration to the future. The board helps relate the institution to its chief community: for example, the community college to serve the educational needs of a defined population area or group, the church-controlled college to be cognizant of the announced position of its denomination, and the comprehensive university to discharge the many duties and to accept the appropriate new challenges which are its concern at the several levels of higher education.

The governing board of an institution of higher education in the United States operates, with few exceptions, as the final institutional authority. Private institutions are established by charters; public institutions are established by constitutional or statutory provisions. In private institutions the board is frequently self-perpetuating; in public colleges and universities the present membership of a board may be asked to suggest candidates for appointment. As a whole and individually, when the governing board confronts the problem of succession, serious attention should be given to obtaining properly qualified persons. Where public law calls for election of governing board members, means should be found to ensure the nomination of fully suited persons, and the electorate should be informed of the relevant criteria for board membership.

Since the membership of the board may embrace both individual and collective competence of recognized weight, its advice or help may be sought through established channels by other components of the academic community. The governing board of an institution of higher education, while maintaining a general overview, entrusts the conduct of administration to the administrative officers–the president and the deans–and the conduct of teaching and research to the faculty. The board should undertake appropriate self-limitation.

One of the governing board's important tasks is to ensure the publication of codified statements that define the overall policies and procedures of the institution under its jurisdiction.

The board plays a central role in relating the likely needs of the future to predictable resources; it has the responsibility for husbanding the endowment; it is responsible for obtaining needed capital and operating funds; and in the broadest sense of the term it should pay attention to personnel policy. In order to fulfill these duties, the board should be aided by, and may insist upon, the development of long-range planning by the administration and faculty. When ignorance or ill will threatens the institution or any part of it, the governing board must be available for support. In grave crises it will be expected to serve as a champion. Although the action to be taken by it will usually be on behalf of the president, the faculty, or the student body, the board should make clear that the protection it offers to an individual or a group is, in fact, a fundamental defense of the vested interests of society in the educational institution.[3]

4. The Academic Institution: The President

The president, as the chief executive officer of an institution of higher education, is measured largely by his or her capacity for institutional leadership. The president shares responsibility for the definition and attainment of goals, for administrative action, and for operating the communications system that links the components of the academic community. The president represents the institution to its many publics. The president's leadership role is supported by delegated authority from the board and faculty.

As the chief planning officer of an institution, the president has a special obligation to innovate and initiate. The degree to which a president can envision new horizons for the institution, and can persuade others to see them and to work toward them, will often constitute the chief measure of the president's administration.

The president must at times, with or without support, infuse new life into a department; relatedly, the president may at times be required, working within the concept of tenure, to solve problems of obsolescence. The president will necessarily utilize the judgments of the faculty but may also, in the interest of academic standards, seek outside evaluations by scholars of acknowledged competence.

It is the duty of the president to see to it that the standards and procedures in operational use within the college or university conform to the policy established by the governing board and to the standards of sound academic practice. It is also incumbent on the president to ensure that faculty views, including dissenting views, are presented to the board in those areas and on those issues where responsibilities are shared. Similarly, the faculty should be informed of the views of the board and the administration on like issues.

The president is largely responsible for the maintenance of existing institutional resources and the creation of new resources; has ultimate managerial responsibility for a large area of nonacademic activities; is responsible for public understanding; and by the nature of the office is the chief person who speaks for the institution. In these and other areas the president's work is to plan, to organize, to direct, and to represent. The presidential function should receive the general support of board and faculty.

5. The Academic Institution: The Faculty

The faculty has primary responsibility for such fundamental areas as curriculum, subject matter and methods of instruction, research, faculty status, and those aspects of student life which relate to the educational process.[4] On these matters the power of review or final decision lodged in the governing board or delegated by it to the president should be exercised adversely only in exceptional circumstances, and for reasons communicated to the faculty. It is desirable that the faculty should, following such communication, have opportunity for further consideration and further transmittal of its views to the president or board. Budgets, personnel limitations, the time element, and the policies of other groups, bodies, and agencies having jurisdiction over the institution may set limits to realization of faculty advice.

The faculty sets the requirements for the degrees offered in course, determines when the requirements have been met, and authorizes the president and board to grant the degrees thus achieved.

Faculty status and related matters are primarily a faculty responsibility; this area includes appointments, reappointments, decisions not to reappoint, promotions, the granting of tenure, and dismissal. The primary responsibility of the faculty for such matters is based upon the fact that its judgment is central to general educational policy. Furthermore, scholars in a particular field or activity have the chief competence for judging the work of their colleagues; in such competence it is implicit that responsibility exists for both adverse and favorable judgments. Likewise, there is the more general competence of experienced faculty personnel committees having a broader charge. Determinations in these matters should first be by faculty action through established procedures, reviewed by the chief academic officers with the concurrence of the board. The governing board and president should, on questions of faculty status, as in other matters where the faculty has primary responsibility, concur with the faculty judgment except in rare instances and for compelling reasons which should be stated in detail.

The faculty should actively participate in the determination of policies and procedures governing salary increases.

The chair or head of a department, who serves as the chief representative of the department within an institution, should be selected either by departmental election or by appointment following consultation with members of the department and of related departments; appointments should normally be in conformity with department members' judgment. The chair or department head should not have tenure in office; tenure as a faculty member is a matter of separate right. The chair or head should serve for a stated term but without prejudice to reelection or to reappointment by procedures that involve appropriate faculty consultation. Board, administration, and faculty should all bear in mind that the department chair or head has a special obligation to build a department strong in scholarship and teaching capacity.

Agencies for faculty participation in the government of the college or university should be established at each level where faculty responsibility is present. An agency should exist for the presentation of the views of the whole faculty. The structure and procedures for faculty participation should be designed, approved, and established by joint action of the components of the institution. Faculty representatives should be selected by the faculty according to procedures determined by the faculty.[5]

The agencies may consist of meetings of all faculty members of a department, school, college, division, or university system, or may take the form of faculty-elected executive committees in departments and schools and a faculty-elected senate or council for larger divisions or the institution as a whole.

The means of communication among the faculty, administration, and governing board now in use include: (1) circulation of memoranda and reports by board committees, the administration, and faculty committees; (2) joint ad hoc committees; (3) standing liaison committees; (4) membership of faculty members on administrative bodies; and (5) membership of faculty members on governing boards. Whatever the channels of communication, they should be clearly understood and observed.

On Student Status

When students in American colleges and universities desire to participate responsibly in the government of the institution they attend, their wish should be recognized as a claim to opportunity both for educational experience and for involvement in the affairs of their college or university. Ways should be found to permit significant student participation within the limits of attainable effectiveness. The obstacles to such participation are large and should not be minimized: inexperience, untested capacity, a transitory status which means that present action does not carry with it subsequent responsibility, and the inescapable fact that the other components of the institution are in a position of judgment over the students. It is important to recognize that student needs are strongly related to educational experience, both formal and informal.

Students expect, and have a right to expect, that the educational process will be structured, that they will be stimulated by it to become independent adults, and that they will have effectively transmitted to them the cultural heritage of the larger society. If institutional support is to have its fullest possible meaning, it should incorporate the strength, freshness of view, and idealism of the student body.

The respect of students for their college or university can be enhanced if they are given at least these opportunities: (1) to be listened to in the classroom without fear of institutional reprisal for the substance of their views, (2) freedom to discuss questions of institutional policy and operation, (3) the right to academic due process when charged with serious violations of institutional regulations, and (4) the same right to hear speakers of their own choice as is enjoyed by other components of the institution.

NOTES

1. See the 1940 "Statement of Principles on Academic Freedom and Tenure," AAUP, Policy Documents and Reports, 11th ed. (Baltimore: *Johns Hopkins University Press,* 2015), 13–19,, and the 1958 "Statement on Procedural Standards in Faculty Dismissal Proceedings," ibid., 91–93. These statements were jointly adopted by the Association of American Colleges (now the Association of American Colleges and Universities) and the American Association of University Professors; the 1940 "Statement" has been endorsed by numerous learned and scientific societies and educational associations.

2. With respect to faculty members, the 1940 "Statement of Principles on Academic Freedom and Tenure" reads: "College and university teachers are citizens, members of a learned profession, and officers of an educational institution. When they speak or write as citizens, they should be free from institutional censorship or discipline, but their special position in the community imposes special obligations. As scholars and educational officers,

they should remember that the public may judge their profession and their institution by their utterances. Hence they should at all times be accurate, should exercise appropriate restraint, should show respect for the opinions of others, and should make every effort to indicate that they are not speaking for the institution" (ibid., 14).

3. Traditionally, governing boards developed within the context of single-campus institutions. In more recent times, governing and coordinating boards have increasingly tended to develop at the multi-campus regional, systemwide, or statewide levels. As influential components of the academic community, these supra-campus bodies bear particular responsibility for protecting the autonomy of individual campuses or institutions under their jurisdiction and for implementing policies of shared responsibility. The American Association of University Professors regards the objectives and practices recommended in the "Statement on Government" as constituting equally appropriate guidelines for such supra-campus bodies, and looks toward continued development of practices that will facilitate application of such guidelines in this new context. [Preceding note adopted by the AAUP's Council in June 1978.]

4. With regard to student admissions, the faculty should have a meaningful role in establishing institutional policies, including the setting of standards for admission, and should be afforded opportunity for oversight of the entire admissions process. [Preceding note adopted by the Council in June 2002.]

5. The American Association of University Professors regards collective bargaining, properly used, as another means of achieving sound academic government. Where there is faculty collective bargaining, the parties should seek to ensure appropriate institutional governance structures which will protect the right of all faculty to participate in institutional governance in accordance with the "Statement on Government." [Preceding note adopted by the Council in June 1978.]

REFERENCES

ACPA, & NASPA. (2015). *Professional competency areas for student affairs educators.* Washington D.C.: Authors. https://www.naspa.org/images/uploads/main/ACPA_NASPA_Professional_Competencies_FINAL.pdf

Alexander, W.M. (1969). Rethinking student government for larger universities. *The Journal of Higher Education, 40*(1), 39–46.

Alves v. Board of Regents of the University System of Georgia, 804 F.3d 1149 (11th Cir. 2015).

American Association of University Professors. (1967). Statement on Government of Colleges and Universities. Washington, DC: Author. https://www.aaup.org/report/statement-government-colleges-and-universities.

American Association of University Professors. (n.d.). *Data snapshot: Contingent faculty in US higher ed.* https://www.aaup.org/sites/default/files/10112018%20Data%20Snapshot%20Tenure.pdf

Amy, J. (2019, May 16). Ole Miss professor slammed over political tweet gets tenure. *U.S. News.* https://www.usnews.com/news/best-states/mississippi/articles/2019-05-16/ole-miss-professor-slammed-on-tweet-gets-tenure-after-debate

Aristotle. (2004). *Rhetoric* (W.R. Roberts, Trans.). Mineola, NY: Dover Publications.

Association of Governing Boards. (2016). *Shared governance: Is OK good enough.* Washington D.C.: Author.

Association of Governing Boards. (2017). *Shared governance: Changing with the times.* Washington D.C.: Author.

Austin, J., & Jones, G.A. (2006). *Governance of higher education: Global perspectives, theories, and practices.* New York: Routledge.

Bahls, S.E. (2014). *Shared governance in time of change: A practical guide for universities and colleges.* Washington, D.C.: Association of Governing Boards.

Barr, M.J., & McClellan, G.S. (2018). *Budgets and financial management in higher education.* San Francisco, CA: Jossey-Bass.

Barrett, M.S., & Quarless, D. (2017). Engaging and keeping faculty and students in governance. In S.F. Cramer (Ed.), *Shared governance in higher education: Demands, transitions, and transformations* (vol. 1, pp. 41–68). Albany, NY: State University of New York Press.

Bauer-Wolf, J. (2019, September 16). Free speech laws mushroom in wake of campus protests. *Inside Higher Ed.* https://www.insidehighered.com/news/2019/09/16/states-passing-laws-protect-college-students-free-speech

Bejou, D., & Bejou, A. (2016). Shared governance: The key to higher education equilibrium. *Journal of Relationship Marketing, 15*(1-2), 54–61.

Benjamin, E. (2013). *How unions strengthen shared governance: A response to a Chronicle opinion piece on unions and shared governance.* Washington, D.C.: American Association of University Professors. https://www.aaup.org/sites/default/files/Unions-Shared-Gov.pdf.

Bentley, E. D. (2016, Feb. 4). *Fair play?* Inside Higher Education. https://www.insidehighered.com/views/2016/02/04/do-college-athletes-have-first-amendment-right-strike-essay

Bess, J., & Dee, J. (2008). *Understanding college and university organization theories for effective policy and practice.* Sterling, VA: Stylus.

Birnbaum, R. (2004). The end of shared governance: Looking ahead or looking back. In W.G. Tierney & V.M. Lechuga (Eds.), *Restructuring shared governance in higher education.* (New Directions in Higher Education, #127, pp. 5–22). San Francisco, CA: Wiley.

Bloland, P.A. (1967). *Student group advising in higher education.* Alexandria, VA: American College Personnel Association.

Blumenstyk, G. (November 11, 2018). Meet the new mega-university. *Chronicle of Higher Education.* https://www.chronicle.com/article/Meet-the-New-Mega-University/245049.

Boyer, E. (1990). *Campus life: In search of community.* San Francisco, CA: The Carnegie Foundation for the Advancement of Teaching.

Bracco, K.R., Richardson, R.C., Callan, P.M., & Finney, J.E. (1999). Policy environment and system designs: Understanding state governance structures. *Review of Higher Education, 23*(1), 23–44.

Bray, N.J. (2006). Effects and assessment of student involvement (pp. 19–32). In M. Miller & D.P. Nadler (Eds.), *Student governance and institutional policy: Formation and implementation.* Greenwich, CT: Information Age Publishing.

Brinbaum, R. (1989). The latent organizational functions of the faculty senate: Why senates do not work but will not got away. *Journal of Higher Education, 60*(4), 423–443.

Brower, R., Jones, T. B., Tandberg, D., Hu, S., & Park, T. (2017). Comprehensive developmental education reform in Florida: A policy implementation typology. *Journal of Higher Education, 88*(6), 809–834. https://doi.org/10.1080/00221546.2016.1272091

Burbules, N.C. (October 28, 2013). How unions weaken shared governance. *Chronicle of Higher Education.* https://www-chronicle-com.umiss.idm.oclc.org/article/How-Unions-Weaken-Shared/142625.

Burgan, M. (2004). Preface. In W.G. Tierney (Ed.), *Competing conceptions of academic governance: Negotiating the perfect storm* (pp. vi–xiv). Baltimore, MD: John Hopkins University Press.

Carnegie Commission on Higher Education. (1973). *Governance of higher education: Six priority problems.* New York: McGraw-Hill.

Carnegie Foundation for the Advancement of Teaching. (1990). *Campus life: In search of community.* Princeton, N.J.: Princeton University Press.

Clark, B.R., & Trow, M. (1966). The organizational context. In T. M. Newcomband & E. K. Wilson (Eds.), *College peer groups: Problems and prospects for research* (pp. 17–70). Chicago: Adline Press.

Cohen, M. & March, J., & Olsen, J. (1972). A garbage can model of choice. *Administrative Science Quarterly, 17*(1), 1-25. https://doi.org/10.2307/2392088

Cohen, M.D., & March, J.G. (1974). *Leadership and ambiguity: The American college president.* New York: McGraw-Hill.

Collis, D.J. (2004). The paradox of scope: A challenge to the governance of higher education. In W.G. Tierney (Ed.), *Competing conceptions of academic governance: Negotiating the perfect storm* (pp. 33–76). Baltimore, MD: John Hopkins University Press.

Corson, J.J. (1960). *Governance of colleges and universities.* New York: McGraw Hill.

Council for the Advancement of Standards. (2015). *CAS professional standards for higher education* (9th ed.). Washington D.C.: Author.

Cowley, W.H. (1980). *Presidents, professors, and trustees.* San Francisco: Jossey Bass.

Cramer, S.F. (2017). Editor's note. In S.F. Cramer (Ed.), *Shared governance in higher education: Demands, transitions, and transformations* (pp. xv–xvi). Albany, NY: State University of New York Press.

Cramer, S.F., & Mozlin, R. (2017). Shared governance: The benefits of systemness. In S.F. Cramer (Ed.), *Shared governance in higher education: Demands, transitions, and transformations* (vol. 1, pp. 89–116). Albany, NY: State University of New York Press.

Crellin, M.A. (2010). The future of shared governance. In M. Kramer (Ed.), *The stress of change: Testing the resilience of institutions.* (New Directions for Higher Education, #151, pp. 71–81). San Francisco, CA: Wiley.

Crow, B.R., & Trow, M. (1966). The organizational context. In T.M. Newcomb & E.K. Wilson (Eds.), *College peer groups: Problems and prospects for research.* Hawthorne, N.Y.: Aldine.

Daniel, J., Kanwar, A., & Uvalic-Trumbic, S. (2005). *Mega-universities = Mega quality?* Address at the 2nd World Summit of Mega-Universities in New Delhi, India on September 25, 2005. http://oasis.col.org/bitstream/handle/11599/1530/2005_Danieletal_MegaUniversityQuality_Transcript.pdf.

Davenport E. (2015). Unionization and shared governance at Historically Black Colleges and Universities. *Thought and Action,* 39–54.

Davis, H.D. (2006). Involvement of student trustees in governance: Tokenism or substance? (pp. 81–91). In M. Miller & D.P. Nadler (Eds.), *Student governance and institutional policy: Formation and implementation.* Greenwich, CT: Information Age Publishing.

De facto. (n.d.). In *Meriam-Webster online dictionary.* Accessed on November 7, 2018 at https://www.meriam-webster.com/dictionary/de facto.

De jure (n.d.). In *Meriam-Webster online dictionary.* Accessed on November 7, 2018 at https://www.meriam-webster.com/dictionary/de facto.

Devins, N. (2008). Congressional responses to judicial decisions. In Mark Graber et al. (Eds.), *Encyclopedia of the Supreme Court* (1st ed., pp. 400–403). MacMillan.

Dimaggio, P.J., & Powell, W.W. (1983). The iron cage revisited: Institutional isomorphism and collective rationality is organizational fields. *American Sociological Review, 49*(2), 147–160.

Dixon v. University of Toledo, 702 F.3d 269 (6th Cir. 2012).

Dudley-Eshbach, J. (March 13, 2011). Shared governance need not be a charade. *Chronicle of Higher Education.* https://www.chronicle.com/article/Shared-Governance-Need-Not-Be/126694.

Ellingson, D.A., Elbert, D.J., & Moser, S. (2010). Advisory councils for business colleges: Composition and utilization. *American Journal of Business Education, 3*(1), 1–8.

Etzioni, A. (1964). *Modern organizations.* Engelwood Cliffs, NJ: Prentice-Hall.

Field, K. (September 23, 2018). In rural Vermont, students are 'reimagining' a college's future. *The Chronicle of Higher Education.* Accessed on September 27 2018 at https://www.chronicle.com/article/At-This-Rural-Vermont-College/244567.

Fish, S. (2007). Shared governance: Democracy is not an educational idea. *Change, 39*(2), 8–13.

Fisher v. University Texas at Austin, 136 S. Ct. 2198 (2016).

Flaherty, C. (2019, September 13). Ruling out grad unions. *Inside Higher Ed.* https://www.insidehighered.com/news/2019/09/23/trump-labor-board-proposes-new-rule-against-grad-unions

Fowler, F. C. (2013). *Policy studies for educational leaders: An introduction* (4th ed.). Pearson.

French, J., & Raven, B.H. (1959). The bases of social power. In D Cartwright (Ed.), *Studies in social power* (pp. 150–167). Ann Arbor, MI: Institute for Social Research.

Ganucheau, A. (2020, June 15). IHL college board to approve relocating Confederate monument from heart of Ole Miss campus. *Mississippi Today.* https://mississippitoday.org/2020/06/15/ihl-college-board-to-approve-relocating-confederate-monument-from-heart-of-ole-miss-campus/

Gerber, L.G. (2014). *The rise and decline of faculty governance: Professionalization and the modern American university.* Baltimore, MD: John Hopkins University Press.

Giddens, A. (1990). *The consequences of modernity.* Stanford, CA: Stanford University Press.

Goldstein Hode, M., Meisenbach, R. J. (2017). Reproducing whiteness through diversity: A critical discourse analysis of the pro-affirmative action amicus briefs in the *Fisher* case. *Journal of Diversity in Higher Education, 10*(2), 162–180. http://dx.doi.org/10.1037/dhe0000014

Goodman, D. (2017). Conclusion: Working together to share governance. In S.F. Cramer (Ed.), *Shared governance in higher education: Demands, transitions, and transformations* (vol. 1, pp. 245–253). Albany, NY: State University of New York Press.

Grutter v. Bollinger, 539 U.S. 306 (2003).

Hall, C. (1962). *Student government: An analysis of its origin and purpose, with the history of The Associated Students of the University of Washington and an analysis of the 1961 ASUW presidential election.* Seattle: Political Science 499.

Hesson, T. (2020, June 1). Trump faces election risks in looming Supreme Court ruling on 'Dreamers,' *Reuters.* https://www.reuters.com/article/us-usa-trump

-immigration-election-analys/trump-faces-election-risks-in-looming-supreme-court-ruling-on-dreamers-idUSKBN238281

Ho, M. (June 14, 2017). What the Purdue-Kaplan deal means for you. *InsideHigherEd.* https://www.insidehighered.com/views/2017/06/14/key-trends-all-institutions-embedded-purdue-kaplan-acquisition-essay.

Hong, J. (October 23, 2017). Graduate students' path to unionization remains rocky. *Chronicle of Higher Education.*

Horvath, V. (2017). Why shared governance is essential for administrators. In S.F. Cramer (Ed.), *Shared governance in higher education: New paradigms, evolving perspectives* (vol. 2, pp. 22–29). Albany, NY: State University of New York Press.

Hurley, L. (2019, October 6). Gay, transgender rights in spotlight as U.S. Supreme Court returns. *Reuters.* https://www.reuters.com/article/us-usa-court-lgbt/gay-transgender-rights-in-spotlight-as-u-s-supreme-court-returns-idUSKCN1WL07F

Hutchens, N. H. (2009). A confused concern of the First Amendment: The uncertain status of constitutional protection for individual academic freedom. *Journal of College and University Law, 36*(1), 145–190.

Hutchens, N. H., & Fernandez, F. (2018). "Flipping" the tenure debate and the continuing need to protect academic freedom. In J. L. DeVitis & P. A. Sasso (Eds.), *Colleges at the crossroads: Taking sides on contested issues.* Bern, Switzerland: Peter Lang Publishing.

Jaschick, S. (2013, July 29). The right to speak out. *Inside Higher Ed.* https://www.insidehighered.com/news/2013/07/29/u-california-board-regents-adopts-new-measure-academic-freedom

Jaschik, S. (2009, November 10). Threat to faculty speech. *Inside Higher Ed.* https://www.insidehighered.com/news/2009/11/10/threat-faculty-free-speech

Johnson, E. (2019, September 9). *Alabama dean resigns following tweets on racism. Inside Higher Ed.* https://www.insidehighered.com/news/2019/09/09/alabama-dean-resigns-following-breitbart-article-tweets

Jones, A., Hutchens, N.H., Hulbert, A., Lewis, W.D., & Brown, D.M. (2017). Shared governance among the new majority: Non-tenure track faculty for eligibility for election to university faculty senates. *Innovative Higher Education, 42*(5-6), 505–519.

Jones, G.A., & Skolnik, M.L. (1997). Governing boards in Canadian universities. *Review of Higher Education, 20*(3), 277–295.

Kane, C. (2017). Advancing student leader development through student organizational advising and institutional support. In D.M. Rosch (Ed.), *The role of student organizations in developing leadership* (New Directions for Student Leadership, 155, 59–70). San Francisco, CA: Wiley.

Kaplin, G.E. (2004). Do governance structures matter? In W.G. Tierney & V.M. Lechuga (Eds.), *Restructuring shared governance in higher education* (New Directions in Higher Education, #127, pp. 23–34). San Francisco, CA: Wiley.

Kaplin, W. A., Lee, B. A., Hutchens, N. H., & Rooksby, J. (2019). *The law of higher education* (6th ed.). San Francisco, CA: Jossey-Bass.

Kater, S., & Levin, J.S. (2004). Shared governance in the community college. *Community College Journal of Research and Practice, 29*(1), 1–23.

Kaufman-Osborn, T.V. (May 26, 2016). The faculty's complicity. *Inside Higher Ed.* https://www.insidehighered.com/views/2016/05/26/faculty-members-play-role-erosion-shared-governance-essay.

Kim v. Regents of Univ. of Cal., 95 Cal. Rptr. 2d 10 (Cal. Ct. App. 2000)

King, K. L., & Leuzinger, J. A. (2015). Introduction to the law and the American legal system. In R. Fossey & S. Eckes (Eds.), *Contemporary issues in higher education Law* (3d ed., pp. 1–21). Education Law Association.

Kingdon, J. W. (2011). *Agendas, alternatives, and public policies* (updated 2nd ed.). Boston, MA: Longman.

Kitchener, K.S. (1984). Intuition, critical evaluation and ethical principles: The foundation for ethical decisions in counseling psychology. *Counseling Psychologist, 12*(3), 43–55.

Klopf, G. (1960). *College student government.* New York: Harper & Brothers.

Kroger, J. (2020, Feb. 9). How to use lawyers. *Inside Higher Ed.* https://www.insidehighered.com/blogs/leadership-higher-education/how-use-lawyers

Kuh, G.D., & Lund, J.P. (1994). What students gain from participating in student government. In M.C. Terrell & M.J. Cuyjet (Eds.), *Developing student government leadership* (New Directions for Student Services, #66, pp. 5–17). San Francisco, CA: Wiley.

Kurtz, G. (Producer), & Lucas, G. (Director). (1977.) *Star Wars.* United States: 20th Century Fox.

Kurtz, S., Manley, J., & Butcher, J. (n.d). *Campus free speech: A legislative proposal.* Goldwater Institute. https://goldwaterinstitute.org/wp-content/uploads/2019/03/Campus-Free-Speech-A-Legislative-Proposal_Web.pdf

LaBanc, B. H., Fernandez, F., Hutchens, N., & Melear, K. B. (2020). *The contested campus.* NASPA.

Labaree, D.F. (1997). Public goods, private goods: The American struggle over education goals. *American Educational Research Journal, 34*(1), pp. 39–81.

Lachs, J. (February 6, 2011). Shared governance is a myth. *Chronicle of Higher Education.* https://www.chronicle.com/article/Shared-Governance-Is-a-Myth/126245.

Lechuga, V.M. (2004). Exploring current issues on shared governance. In W.G. Tierney & V.M. Lechuga (Eds.), *Restructuring shared governance in higher education* (New Directions in Higher Education, #127, pp. 95–98). San Francisco, CA: Wiley.

Levin, J.S. (2009). Institutional governance and the interests of students. In G.S. McClellan & J. Stringer (Eds.), *The handbook of student affairs administration* (3rd ed., pp. 45–64). San Francisco, CA: Jossey Bass.

Lingenfelter, P.E. (2004). The state and higher education: An essential partnership. In W.G. Tierney & V.M. Lechuga (Eds.), *Restructuring shared governance in higher education* (New Directions in Higher Education, #127, pp. 47–59). San Francisco, CA: Wiley.

Little, J., & Lee, B. (Producers). (2000). *Bruce Lee: A Warrior's Journey.* [Documentary]. China: Warner Home Studio.

Lizzio, A., & Wilson, K. (2009). Student participation in university governance: The role conceptions and sense of efficacy of student representatives on departmental committees. *Studies in Higher Education, 34*(1), 69–84.

Lloyd, W.F. (1833). *Two lectures on the checks to population.* England: Oxford University. https://archive.org/details/twolecturesonch00lloygoog/page/n5.

Lodge, C. (2005). From hearing voices to engaging in dialogue: Problematizing student participation in school improvement. *Journal of Educational Change, 6,* 125–146.

Lubbers, J. S. (2018). *A guide to federal agency rulemaking* (6th ed.). American Bar Association.

Lucey, C.A. (2002). Civic engagement, shared governance, and community colleges. *Academe, 88*(4), 27–32.

Marginson, S. (2004). Going global: Governance implications of cross-border traffic in higher education. In W.G. Tierney (Ed.), *Competing conceptions of academic governance: Negotiating the perfect storm* (pp. 1–32). Baltimore, MD: John Hopkins University Press.

Marting, R. (2003). The problem with student and faculty trustees. *Trusteeship, 11*(4), 29–32.

Mayhew, L.B. (1974). *Administration and governance of the university.* Unpublished manuscript.

Miles, J.M., & Miller, M.T. (2006). Increasing student participation in self-governance: The recommendations of student leaders (pp. 69–79). In M. Miller & D.P. Nadler (Eds.), *Student governance and institutional policy: Formation and implementation.* Greenwich, CT: Information Age Publishing.

Miller, G. S. (2019). Choose your friends wisely: How organizational identity influences behavior at U.S. colleges and universities. *Review of Higher Education, 42*(3), 1185–1206. https://doi.org/10.1353/rhe.2019.0033

Miller, M. (2003). *Improving faculty governance.* Stillwater, OK: New Forums.

Miller, M., & Nadler, D. P. (2006a). Introduction (pp. xi–xii). In M. Miller & D.P. Nadler (Eds.), *Student governance and institutional policy: Formation and implementation.* Greenwich, CT: Information Age Publishing.

Miller, M., & Nadler, D. P. (2006b). Student involvement in governance: Rationale, problems, and opportunities (pp. 9–18). In M. Miller & D.P. Nadler (Eds.), *Student governance and institutional policy: Formation and implementation.* Greenwich, CT: Information Age Publishing.

Miller, M.T., Smith, E.A., & Nadler, D.P. (2016). Debate and discourse: The role of the faculty senate on the modern American campus. *Journal of Higher Education Theory and Practice, 16*(3), 22–29.

Mix, V.L. (2013). Library and university governance: Partners in student success. *Reference Services Review, 41*(2), 253–265.

Morgan, G. (2006). *Images of organization* (3rd ed.). Thousand Oaks, CA: Sage.

Murdock, J. (2006). Putting it all together (pp. 117-122). In M. Miller & D.P. Nadler (Eds.), *Student governance and institutional policy: Formation and implementation.* Greenwich, CT: Information Age Publishing.

Nagai, J., & Nehls, K. (2013). Non-alumni advisory board volunteers. *Innovative Higher Education, 39*(1), 3–16.

National Center for Educational Statistics. (2001). *Table 244: Degree-granting institutions, by control and type of institutions: 1949–50 to 2000–01.* Washington DC: United States Department of Education. https://nces.ed.gov/programs/digest/d01/dt244.asp.

National Center for State Courts. (n.d.). *Appellate procedure: Resource guide.* https://www.ncsc.org/Topics/Appellate/Appellate-Procedure/Resource-Guide.aspx

New, J. (February 11, 2016). Get ready for more protests. *Inside Higher Ed.* https://www.insidehighered.com/news/2016/02/11/survey-finds-nearly-1-10-freshmen-plan-participating-campus-protests.

Nilsen, E., & Zhou, L. (2020, June 8). Democrats' sweeping new police reform bill, explained. *Vox.* https://www.vox.com/2020/6/8/21283841/democrats-police-reform-bill-explained-george-floyd

O'Neill, T. (1995). *All politics is local and other rules of the game.* Avon, MA: Adams Media.

Office of the Federal Registrar. (n.d.). *A guide to the rulemaking process.* https://www.federalregister.gov/uploads/2011/01/the_rulemaking_process.pdf

Okrent, D. (2010). *Last call: The rise and fall of prohibition.* New York, NY: Scribner.

Olson, G.A. (2009, July 23). Exactly what is shared governance? *Chronicle of Higher Education.* https://www.chronicle.com/article/Exactly-What-Is-Shared/47065.

Penrose, M. (2014). Sharing Stupid $h*t with friend and followers: The First Amendment rights of college athletes to use social media. *Southern Methodist University Science & Technology Law Review, 17,* 449–488.

Politics [Def. 1-5]. (n.d.). In *Merriam Webster Online.* Accessed on December 29, 2018 at nary/politics.

Pope, M.L. (2004). A conceptual framework of faculty trust and participation in governance. In W.G. Tierney & V.M. Lechuga (Eds.), *Restructuring shared governance in higher education* (New Directions in Higher Education, #127, pp. 75–84). San Francisco, CA: Wiley.

Porter, S.R. (2013). The causal effect of faculty unions on institutional decision-making. *ILRReview, 66*(5), 1192–1211.

Pusser, B., & Loss, C.P. (2018). *Colleges and organizational structure of universities–Governing boards, the president, faculty, administration and staff, students, future prospects.* http://education.stateuniversity.com/pages/1859/Colleges-Universities-Organizational-Structure.html.

Quarless, D., & Barrett, M.S. (2017). Governance structures: Perspective on administrative task forces in shared governance. In S.F. Cramer (Ed.), *Shared governance in higher education: Demands, transitions, and transformations* (vol. 1, pp. 117–152). Albany, NY: State University of New York Press.

Raven, B.H. (1965). Social influence and power. In I.D. Steiner & M. Fishbein (Eds.), *Current studies in social psychology* (pp. 371–382). New York: Holt, Rinehart, Winston.

Reed, M. (2017). Community colleges, shared governance, and democracy. *Professional Symposium,* April 2017, 428–429

Rhoades, G. (2011). Faculty unions, business models, and the academy's future. *Change, 43*(6), 20–26.

Rosenberg, M., & McCullough, B.C. (1981). Mattering: Inferred significance and mental health among adolescents. *Research in Community & Mental Health, 2,* 163–182.

Ryan, D. (2017). Shared governance and faculty-student partnerships: A history. In S.F. Cramer (Ed.), *Shared governance in higher education: Demands, transitions, and transformations* (vol. 1, pp. 71–72). Albany, NY: State University of New York Press.

Sabatier, P. (2007). The need for better theories. In P. Sabatier (Ed.), *Theories of the policy process* (2nd ed.). Boulder, CO: Westview Press.

Schotz, G. (2007). *What is shared governance anyway?* Washington, D.C.: American Association of University Professors. http://www.cary-nelson.org/AAUP-Resources/Principles/shared_gov_07.pdf.

Schuster, J.H., Smith, D.G., Corak, K.A. & Yamada, M.M. (1994). *Strategic governance.* Phoenix, AZ: American Council on Education.

Silverman, J. (September, 25, 2000). Remember the five basic elements of persuasion. *Albany Business Review.* https://www.bizjournals.com/albany/stories/2000/09/25/smallb5.html.

Simon, H.A. (956). Rational choice and the structure of the environment. *Psychological Review, 63*(2), 129–138.

Spring, H.P. (1944). *What is truth?* Berlin, Germany: Orange Press.

Strange, C.C., & Banning, J.H. (2001). *Educating by design: Creating campus learning environments that work.* San Francisco, CA: Jossey-Bass.

Strauss, B. (August 17, 2015). N.L.R.B. rejects Northwestern football players' unionization bid. *The New York Times.*

Sun, J. C., & McClellan, G. (2020). *Student clashes on campus: A leadership guide to free speech.* London, UK: Routledge.

Taylor, J.S., & De Lourdes Machado, M. (2008). Governing boards in public higher education institutions: A perspective from the United States. *Tertiary Education and Management, 14*(3), 243–260.

Taylor, M. (2013). Shared governance in the modern university. *Higher Education Quarterly, 67*(1), 80–94.

Thelin, J. (2019). *A history of American higher education* (3d ed.). Johns Hopkins University Press.

Thelin, J.R., Edwards, J.R., & Moyen, E. (2018). *Higher education in the United States, historical development.* StateUniversity.com. http://education.stateuniversity.com/pages/2044/Higher-Education-in-United-States.html.

Tierney, W.G. (2003). *Academic vantage points: Reflection on the university in the 21st century.* Center for Higher Education Policy Analysis, University of Southern California.

Tinto, V. (1993). *Leaving college: Rethinking the causes and cures of student attrition* (2nd ed.). Chicago: University of Chicago Press.

United States Department of Education. (n.d.). *How the Office for Civil Rights handles complaints.* https://www2.ed.gov/about/offices/list/ocr/complaints-how.html

United States Student Association. (1980). *History*. Washington D.C.: Author. Accessed on August 28, 2018 at http://usstudents.org/about/history/.

Venable, W., & Gardiner, J.J. (1988). *Synergistic governance, leadership teams, and the academic department head*. Annual meeting of the Association for the Study of Higher Education. St. Louis, MO.

Vroom, V.H. (1964). *Work and motivation*. New York: Wiley.

Wagner, J.W. (2007). Multiversity or university? *The Intellectual Community, 9*(4). http://www.emory.edu/ACAD_EXCHANGE/2007/febmar/wagneressay.html.

Weber, M. (1947). *The theory of social and economic organization*. New York: Free Press.

Weber, M. (1958). *From Max Weber: Essays in sociology*. New York: Oxford University Press.

Weible, C. M., & Sabatier, P. A. (2018) (Eds.). *Theories of the policy process* (4th ed.). London, UK: Routledge.

Wells, R. (2008). Social and cultural capital, race and ethnicity, and college student retention. *Journal of College Student Retention: Research, Theory, & Practice, 10*(2), 103–128.

Wickens, C.M. (2008). The organizational impact of university labor unions. *Higher Education, 56*, 545–564.

Wilensky, H.L. (1964). The professionalization of everyone? *American Journal of Sociology, 70*(2), 137-158.

Winn, M., Sergent, J., & Madhani, A.., & Penzenstadler, N. (2019, July 17). Copy, paste, legislate. *USA Today*. https://www.usatoday.com/pages/interactives/asbestos-sharia-law-model-bills-lobbyists-special-interests-influence-state-laws/

Worth, M. (2008). *Sounding boards: Advisory councils in higher education*. Washington, DC: Association of Governing Boards of Universities and Colleges.

Zaleznik, A. (May 1970). Power and politics in organizational life. *Havard Business Review*. https://hbr.org/1970/05/power-and-politics-in-organizational-life.

Zou, B., & Ratosy, E.W. (1999). Student participation in university governance. *Canadian Journal of Higher Education, 29*(1), 1–26.

Zucker, L.G. (1986). Production of trust: Institutional sources of economic structure, 1840–1920. In B.M. Straw & L.L. Cummings (Eds.), *Research in organizational behavior* (Vol. 8, pp. 53–111). Greenwich, CT: JAI.

INDEX

K

L

M

N

O

ABOUT THE AUTHORS

George S. McClellan is Associate Professor of Higher Education at the University of Mississippi. Prior to joining the students and colleagues at Ole Miss, he served for ten years as the vice chancellor for student affairs at Indiana University–Purdue University Fort Wayne (IPFW). McClellan has also held the position of vice president for student development at Dickinson State University in Dickinson, North Dakota and has supported students in a variety of roles at the University of Arizona and Northwestern University.

He is the (co)author or (co)editor of numerous books, chapters, and articles on student affairs and higher education. His books and monographs include *A Good Job: Campus Employment as High Impact Practice* (2018) with K. Creager and M. Savoca, *Budgets and Financial Management in Higher Education* (2011 & 2018) with Margaret Barr, *The Handbook for Student Affairs Administration* with J. Stringer (2009 & 2016), *Making Change Happen in Student Affairs: Challenges and Strategies* with M. Barr and A. Sandeen (2014), *The Handbook for College Athletics and Recreation Administration* with C. King and D. Rockey, Jr. (2012), *Stepping Up and Stepping Out: Helping Students Transition of the Real World* with J. Parker (2012), *In Search of Safer Communities: Emerging Practices for Student Affairs in Addressing Campus Violence* with M. Jablonski, E. Zdziarksi, D. Ambler,, R. Barnett-Terry, L. Cook, J. Dunkle, R. Gatti, E. Griego, and J. Kindle (New Directions in Student Services, 2008), *Gambling on Campus* with T. Hardy and J. Caswell (New Directions in Student Services, 2006), and *Serving Native American Students* with M. Fox and S. Lowe (New Directions in Student Services, 2005).

McClellan has served in a number leadership positions in student affairs professional associations. He was a member of the editorial board of both the *Journal of College Student Development* and the *Journal of College and Character.* He received the Outstanding Contribution to Research in American Indian Higher Education award from the Native American Network of the American College Personnel Association in 2002 and the Annuit Coeptis Senior Scholar Award from that association in 2017. McClellan served as a member of the National Association of Student Personnel Administrators (NASPA) Foundation Board, a founding member of that NASPA's Administrators in Graduate and Professional Student Services Community and its Indigenous Peoples Knowledge Community, and as chair or co-chair of that association's Task Force on Gambling and its Ad Hoc Work Group on the Voluntary System of Accountability. He was recognized by the NASPA Foundation as a Pillar of the Profession in 2010.

McClellan, a frequent presenter, speaker, and consultant on a variety of topics in student affairs and higher education, received his Ph.D. in Higher Education from the University of Arizona (2003). Both his M.S.Ed. in Higher Education (1998) and B.A. in English and American Literature (1982) were earned from Northwestern University.

Neal Hutchens serves as Professor and Chair in the University of Mississippi School of Education's Department of Higher Education. Hutchens' scholarship focuses on intersections of higher education law and policy and practice. His previous faculty positions include appointments at Penn State University and the University of Kentucky. A key strand of his research has considered issues dealing with free speech and expression in higher education and related issues, such as the inclusion of non-tenure-track faculty members in shared governance structures. Hutchens was the 2015 recipient of the William A. Kaplin Award from the Center for Excellence in Higher Education Law and Policy at Stetson University College of Law. The award is intended to recognize nationally leading scholars whose work embraces intersections of law and policy.

Hutchens' scholarship has appeared in publications that include the *University of Pennsylvania Journal of Constitutional Law, Journal of College and University Law, Counselor Education and Supervision, Kentucky Law Journal, West's Education Law Reporter, Journal of Law and Education, Innovative Higher Education,* and *Journal of Student Affairs Research and Practice.* Additionally, Hutchens has authored or (co)authored numerous book chapters. He has also written pieces for *The Conversation, The Hechinger Report,* NASPA's *Leadership Exchange, The Chronicle of Higher Education,* and *Inside Higher Ed.*

Hutchens is on the author team–along with William A. Kaplin, Barbara A. Lee, and Jacob H. Rooksby–for the sixth edition of *The Law of Higher Education,* the preeminent treatise on higher education law. Along with Brandi Hephner LaBanc, Frank Fernandez, and Kerry Brian Melear, he is (co)author of *The Contested Campus: Aligning Professional Values, Social Justice, Free Speech* published by NASPA.

Hutchens has served on the editorial board for *The Review of Higher Education.* He is currently a reviewer for *Education Law & Policy Review,* a member of the authors' committee for *West's Education Law Reporter,* and an editorial board member for the *Journal of College and University Law.* He also serves on the Litigation Committee for the American Association of University Professors and is a past board member of the Education Law Association.

Hutchens earned his Ph.D. from the University of Maryland and his J.D. from the University of Alabama School of Law, where he graduated *summa cum laude* and was a member of the Order of the Coif and of the *Alabama Law Review.*